HOW TO WRITE
Irresistible
QUERY
LETTERS

Lisa Collier Cool

WRITER'S DIGEST BOOKS
Cincinnati, Ohio

Library of Congress Cataloging-in-Publication Data

Cool, Lisa Collier
   How to write irresistible query letters.
   Includes Index.
   1. Queries (Authorship) I. Title.
PN161.C66   1987   808'.02   87-2085
ISBN 0-89879-391-2

Design by Quarasan Publishing Services.

To my twin inspirations Alison and Georgia,
and my husband, John

$\boxed{A}$cknowledgments

For their contributions to this book, I'd like to thank:

Maxine Abrams; Robert Elgin; Rory Foster, DVM; William Hoffman; Susan Lapinski; Catherine Lilly, Ph.D.; Daniel Martin, Ph.D.; L. Scott Morgan; Amy Sunshine-Genova; and Elizabeth Tener for allowing me to reproduce their queries.

Oscar Collier, my father and agent, for his encouragement and valuable advice.

The courteous and helpful librarians at the New Rochelle Library for their research pointers.

Jean Fredette for her editorial expertise.

*T*able of Contents

Introduction: Profitable Paragraphs   1

If you master the art of writing the query letter to a magazine or book publisher—the author's personalized sales pitch—your next sale may be just a few well chosen, easy-to-write paragraphs away.

How to Use This Book   3

Check this quick guide to each section of the book before you begin your query.

1. Ideas That Sell   4

Strategies for recognizing and developing saleable ideas for some of the approximately one million articles magazine editors need annually.

2. Secrets of Successful Slanting   14

How to narrow down a too-general, too-big book or magazine topic into a sub-category or a new or special focus that can be explored in detail.

3. Leads That Hook the Editor   25

Effective query openers to get and keep an editor's attention—and that can later begin your article or book.

4. Tantalizing Descriptions   36

After your lead, how to make your subsequent query summary succinct, including pertinent information on your writing, research and publishing process of interest to the editor.

5. Selling Yourself   46

What to include, what not to include in your author's bio, and how to highlight the writing-related experience that best shows your qualifications for the job.

6. Research and Interview Shortcuts 55

The most effective research and interview methods to keep your query preparation at a profitable minimum.

7. Letter Perfect 63

The final steps to making your query professional: keep it concise, organize and clarify, sharpen your style and proofread for accuracy.

8. Querying Agents and Book Publishers 75

How to structure the longer and more complex book query that must include the nuts and bolts of your approach plus potential target audiences, sales points, promotion plans and possible subsidiary rights.

9. A Rogue's Gallery 88

Rejection-proof your query to avoid these common, subtle mistakes and inappropriate phrases and tenses that may sabotage a good book or article idea.

10. Strategic Submissions 94

A checklist for successful query submissions: understanding the markets, book contracts, rights, and single and multiple submissions.

11. Anatomy of a Winner 110

The dissection of successful queries of beginning and established writers, illustrating the effective techniques that have produced sales.

12. Power Querying 128

How to develop a working image, a credible track record, and think and plan *big* for future sales and a steady income.

Index 135

$\boxed{I}$ ntroduction

Profitable Paragraphs

How can you make a five-hundred-dollar or one-thousand-dollar magazine article sale, just by investing the time it takes to write a letter? Grab the attention of a top literary agent with a few well chosen words—or sell your *unwritten* nonfiction book yourself, for five thousand dollars, fifteen thousand dollars or more?

A query letter—a combination sales pitch and nonfiction article or book summary—can do all this and more. Not just for the established pro, queries can work for any writer. As a literary agent and writing teacher, I've seen unpublished writers crack top markets like *Glamour, Cosmopolitan, Savvy,* and *Harper's* with magazine queries.

Selling by query, rather than with a complete manuscript, is the most profitable way to write. With your one- or two-page letter, you can get an idea before editors without spending days or weeks researching, writing, and polishing a piece that might turn out to be unsaleable. And in the time you'd have spent on that one piece, you could write and submit *several* queries, multiplying your sales prospects substantially.

Queries increase the number of potential markets you can hit, too. They're cheaper to submit, and with minor revisions, your basic query letter can be quickly "personalized" for many different publishers—a laborious task with a completed article. A good idea could produce several sales, allowing you to get more mileage out of your research and interviewing time. And with a few credits on the subject, you can command better prices in the future as an expert on the topic.

Queries won't work for every article subject—send the completed article rather than a query when marketing humor, newspaper pieces, editorials or opinions, or short articles (four typewritten pages or less). But for most of your work, queries are the best marketing approach. Not only do they allow wider submissions and produce faster editorial responses than articles, but they enhance the odds of a sale. While editors often feel reluctant to suggest a rewrite of a finished piece that doesn't quite work for their magazine, a query encourages constructive editorial input. A recent query of mine, on "Glamour Jobs," produced an assignment from *Cosmopolitan* to write on "What's New in Modeling," an approach I hadn't considered.

Even when the query subject doesn't appeal to an editor, an assignment can still result from the submission. The "Glamour Jobs" query produced an assignment from *Playgirl* to write on "Romance in the '80s"—a topic not even touched on in my query letter. Though I have yet to sell "Glamour Jobs," that query has produced thousands of dollars' worth of assignments. A powerfully written query is like a good resume; it sells editors on *you,* not necessarily a particular project.

Mastering the written sales pitch—your query letter—is easy. In this book, I'll tell you exactly how to write the three key sections of any query letter, and I'll reveal the winning formula that I've used to sell dozens of my own articles—as well as *this* book. I'll also share the secrets of both newly published and experienced writers by printing and dissecting their successful queries. Then I'll show you the submission strategies I've succeeded with during my fifteen years as a literary agent and writer.

What's worked for me and many other writers can work for you. With the right query letter, your next sale may be just a few easy-to-write paragraphs away.

HOW TO USE THIS BOOK

This book is organized for easy reference in composing your query. Here's a quick guide to what each section will do for you:

Ideas: Chapters 1 and 2 will help you identify saleable ideas and focus them to meet specific editors' needs.

Writing the Query: Chapters 3, 4, and 5 contain guidelines on composing the three key sections of your query: the lead, summary, and author's biography. Chapter 11 reveals the winning formulas favored by professional writers. For book queries and queries to agents, consult chapter 8.

Facts and Quotes: Chapter 6 will assist you in your research and show you how to conduct interviews with your sources.

Editing and Submitting: Chapter 7 describes how to format and polish the query; chapter 9 alerts you to common query pitfalls to avoid. Chapter 10 details submission strategies, negotiation, and book and magazine contracts.

Chapter 1

Ideas That Sell

> Wanted: one million ideas a year. Payment: $5 to $5,000 per idea.

This imaginary ad sums up the current demand for magazine ideas in the United States. Approximately two million magazine articles are published each year in America's sixteen thousand magazines. Assuming that half are staff-written, that leaves one million possible article sales for freelancers. And each of these sales starts with an idea.

But where do you find the ideas that will sell? Many starting writers complain of difficulty in finding good topics. Frequently the problem is failing to *recognize* saleable ideas when they come along. In my writing classes, students often drop casual references to some fascinating experience or esoteric knowledge of theirs, yet seem astonished when I suggest they write a query on it. "Oh, who'd care about my skydiving experiences?" said one, while another wondered if losing two hundred pounds was really *that* extraordinary. Even a more experienced writer can exhibit this myopia; when a journalist friend happened to mention his rather novel hobby, I realized that where he saw recreation, I saw money—a potential twenty-five-thousand-dollar book contract.

Why didn't these good ideas register on their creators? My theory is that there's a kind of taboo about talking too much about yourself, which in turn makes some writers discount the inherent interest of their own experiences. "Who'd want to read about me?" the writer asks himself—murdering dozens of terrific article topics in their infancy. Actually, the personal touch can be what turns a good article into an excellent one, by increasing readers' involvement in the story.

PROFIT FROM PERSONAL EXPERIENCE

Right now you are probably living several good article ideas; further ideas can be unearthed from your past and immediate future. Consider the jobs you've held, for example. There may be an unusual profession in there: "Laughing All the Way to the Bank—My Six Weeks as a Clown"; a lesson to be learned: "Being Turned Down for Credit Turned Out to Be the Best Thing That Ever Happened to Me"; a strategy others can benefit from: "How I Parlayed Bad Debts into a $500,000 Business." And what about your personal life? Potential article ideas could be lurking in your romantic or sexual experiences, childrearing practices, hobbies, medical history, vacations and recreational activities, even your feelings and emotions.

Use these strategies to capitalize on personal experiences:

Identify Potentially Saleable Experiences.   The most saleable kinds of personal experiences tell a story others can easily relate to. They might be humorous: "Anybody Want a Used Gerbil?" might ruefully recount your problems with kids and pets; inspiring: "A 40-Year-Old Returns to College"; sexy: "My Adventures Working for an Escort Service"; adventurous: "What Was I Doing Dangling Over the Edge of a 50-Foot Cliff?"; practical: "How I Saved $100,000 in Mortgage Payments"; medical: "I'm Having the Baby Doctors Said I'd Never Have"; bizarre: "A Computer Had Me Arrested"; tragic: "When My Lover Died, I Had to Learn to Live Again"; or cautionary: "My House Was Poisoned."

Use Yourself as a Starting Point.   Your own experiences might be included as part of a larger story. When writer Paula Dranov discovered that, like one in five women, she had fibroid tumors, she researched the subject thoroughly, then wrote "What You Should Know About Fibroid Tumors" for *Ladies' Home Journal*, devoting only a few paragraphs to her own case, the rest to up-to-date medical information on the subject. Of the many medical articles Dranov has written, this one attracted the greatest reader response. Similarly, you could turn problems to profit with such articles as "What Every New Homeowner Should Know About Insurance," "New Help for the Colicky Baby," "Avoiding Wedding Mishaps," "When a Spouse is Unfaithful," "Telephone Scams," and "Surviving a Tax Audit."

Live Your Fantasies.   Always wanted to check out videodating services? Curious about European health spas? Wondering what it's like to chauffeur the rich around? Daydreaming about playing on a major league team? With an article or book query, these can be *possible* dreams financed by your publisher. A rich tradition in articles and books is to step into someone else's shoes briefly, then write about it: Gloria Steinem was briefly a Playboy bunny and wrote a successful article, which later became a movie about her experiences; George Plimpton has made a career of playing at being a professional athlete.

But you don't have to *live* your work. You can easily turn the question of "what if" into an article through research. Wish you could pick up some extra income with a second job, but lack the energy? Let your fingers do the walking at the library, then write "Moonlighting Could Become You—and Your Bank Balance," describing some of the more offbeat ways to make ends meet. Just about anything you like to think about could be an interesting article.

Tell Somebody Else's Story.   Has a friend, relative, or acquaintance just won the lottery, delivered quintuplets, started a successful campaign against teen drinking, turned an invention into a thriving business, been the victim of a violent crime, discovered a way to dress well on $150 a year, exposed a scheme to dump hazardous waste in your area, or bought a nice piece of real estate for $1 at a municipal auction? Any of these or hundreds of other adventures could be the basis of an "as told to," first-person account written by you. Or write up the material in the third person as a human interest story. Especially if you live outside of New York City (where most major magazines are situated), consider whether local news could make a national story: "The Woman Who Battled City Hall and Won," "The Town with a Heart," "The Strange Case of Dr. Smith.'

You Can Profit From Profiles and Interviews.   Do you know a few unforgettable characters? Give an unknown the star treatment with a profile or interview piece. Many magazines are interested in business success stories, whether of teenaged tycoons, housewife entrepreneurs, self-made millionaires, inventors, sharp practitioners, or *Fortune* 500 executives. Or you could profile a table tennis hustler, a horror movie star, a top auctioneer, a new wave architect, the doorkeeper of a popular area nightspot, a third-party Presidential candidate, a zookeeper, or anyone else with a colorful, exciting lifestyle or profession. The illustration on page 13 shows a typical query for a profile article.

Or combine several profiles into one article: "The New Mom-

and-Pop Business Owners," "Baby Models," or "Sports Car Designers."

BEST BETS TO SELL

For further inspiration, look over this list of popular article types:

Seasonal.   For every season, there's a sale. Many magazines are eagerly looking for fresh, seasonal article ideas to tie into Christmas/ Hanukkah, Thanksgiving, Easter, the Fourth of July, Mother's and Father's Day, and other holidays. Anniversary articles can also be saleable: "Boston's 200th Birthday," "Gearing Up for the Bimillennium," "Pearl Harbor Remembered." For other holiday and anniversary ideas, consult *Chase's Calendar of Annual Events* (available at many libraries or bookstores), which lists dates for such occasions as Twins Day. Submit seasonal and anniversary ideas at least eight months before the occasion.

Self-Help.   A staple of many women's magazines, and also good for sports and fitness publications, the emotional self-help article tells the reader how to overcome common or uncommon psychological problems that may be holding her (not *him*—men's magazines run very few self-help pieces) back: "Dare to Succeed," "Overcoming Shyness," "What's Another Word for Mom? Guilt," "Developing Willpower." Keys to selling this type of piece are pinpointing a specific problem, quoting psychologists and other authorities, and offering some original solutions to the problem.

How-To.   Good for just about any commercial magazine, depending on the topic, the how-to piece offers step-by-step instructions on a specific subject: "How to Slash Food Bills," "How to Select a Career Counselor," "How to Recognize a Fine Cigar," "How to Catch Brook Trout." The easiest kind of how-to article to sell is one that promises a very specific benefit: "How to Make Your Children Eager Readers," rather than vague advice such as "How to Be a Better Parent."

Career Advice.   Suitable for both men's and women's magazines, the career piece offers the reader strategies on achieving some career goal, overcoming a common job difficulty, changing careers, or doing his or her present job more effectively. Examples include: "The 12 Best Jobs in the Computer Biz," "Coming Off like a Winner at a Job Interview," "How to Get Promoted," and "Avoiding Career Burnout."

Sex Advice.   An almost surefire seller, sex lends itself to a variety of article ideas. You could discuss specific problems: "New Treatments for Impotence" or "The Sexually Stingy Lover"; suggest techniques: "When Your Sexual Styles Don't Mesh"; discuss clinical discoveries: "What We Now Know About Female Orgasm" or "The G-Spot Controversy"; offer practical guidance: "Safe Sex During Pregnancy"; or relate sex to relationship issues: "Is Your Bedroom a Battle Zone?"

Relationships.   Readers are always interested in ideas on improving relationships with children, lovers or spouses, friends, and family members. Possible articles include "Disciplining With Love," "Have an Affair with Your Spouse," "The Blended Family—His Children, Hers, and Theirs," "When a Friend Borrows Money," and "The Impossible In-Law." Or tell the reader how to form interesting *new* relationships: "Where the Boys Are," "High-Tech Matchmakers," or "Turn a Friend Into a Lover."

Personal Finance.   Another perennially interesting topic is money. Articles could cover investment strategies: "High Profits from High-Tech Stock" or "Selecting the Right Mutual Fund"; money management: "Escaping the Plastic Prison" or "Protecting Your Credit Rating"; thrift: "Feed Your Family on $50 a Month" or "Getting a Down Payment on the House of Your Dreams"; avoiding consumer frauds: "Ten Credit Card Scams to Avoid" and "When Your Bank Card is Stolen"; and ways to get better buys.

Exposé.   The favorite article type for men's magazines, investigative pieces give the lowdown on shady land deals, medical frauds and malpractice, government boondoggles, sinister scientific or technological developments, legislative injustices, and other shocking developments on the current scene. Exposés pay well, but they require meticulous research and extreme care in presenting facts (to avoid potentially costly libel suits).

Medical. As America grows more health-conscious, demand for popular medical pieces is increasing. These could be either personal experience—"The Operation That Saved My Husband's Life"—or straight reportage: "Genetic Counseling," "New Treatments for Breast Cancer," "Stress—Its Surprising Benefits." In selecting medical topics, avoid "trendy" diseases such as bulimia, anorexia nervosa, and hypoglycemia—all of which have had extensive magazine and newspaper coverage—unless you have a dramatic new angle or unique approach.

The most saleable ideas are updates on treatments and theories about common health problems: "New Research on the Cold"; technological advances in medicine: "The Fertility Pump"; dramatic true stories of amazing recoveries from serious illnesses; coverage of pregnancy or childhood illness: "Miscarriage—Causes and Prevention"; and general-interest fitness or diet pieces: "The 12 Most Common Exercise Mistakes."

Science and Technology. The lay public is hungry for readable articles on scientific or technological breakthroughs. Write about what's going on right now—"The Electronic Classroom"—or speculate on the implications of current research: "Are Pheromones the Ultimate Aphrodisiac?" For an even more provocative article, translate current findings into futuristic scenarios: "Will the Workers of the Year 2000 Face Genetic Discrimination?"

True Crime. Dramatic recountings of sensational crimes, past or present, can make for gripping reading—and lively writing. Good crime stories include "blood and money" murder cases, unsolved crimes of the past, mysterious disappearances, compelling evidence that some miscarriage of justice has occurred, bizarre crimes, and serial murders. Or do an investigative piece on some current trend in crime: "Terrorist Training Camps in the United States," "Child Snatching—A National Epidemic," or "The Abused Spouse." A well written crime article can possibly be the start of a financial killing of your own, with a book deal or even a movie or TV miniseries.

Lifestyles and Current Trends. Are you a trendsetter among your friends and associates? While relatively few magazines are genuinely avant-garde, many popular publications catering to readers eighteen to thirty years old like to cover the new trends and lifestyles as they start to catch on. Good timing is the key to sales: as soon as you sense a new current rippling through American life, get your query out *fast*. Don't wait for your discovery to become a national mania, or you'll find that the assignments have already been given out.

Travel and Recreation.   Turn your vacations, hobbies, and leisure time activities into profitable article assignments. Not only are there a number of magazines devoted to specific hobbies, forms of recreation, and travel, but most popular magazines cover these topics as well. For large-circulation magazines, budget travel and crafts are the best bets; for more upscale publications, exotic locations and trendy activities are more saleable. Or offer practical advice: "Profiting from Miniatures," "Antiques You Can Buy for Less Than $100", "Untangling the Airfare Maze."

Tragedy and Inspirational Articles.   Reach out and touch a reader's heart by sharing a sad experience; provide a message of hope with an uplifting story of courage, faith, or perseverance; or show that charity, kindness, and decency are still valued. Your piece might take the form of a profile: "A Special Santa"; a human interest piece: "They Climbed Mount Everest—in Wheelchairs"; compassionate advice: "When A Parent Dies"; a personal experience: "My Long Road Back Home"; or a religious theme: "Thy Brother's Keeper."

Evergreens.   Frequently, students of mine come up with good article subjects, but become downcast when another student observes that "it's been done before." However, most nonfiction writing merely builds on what has gone before, rather than breaking completely fresh ground. The classic definition of an evergreen idea is that it touches on fundamental human drives or concerns, such as avoiding danger; preserving health; satisfying hunger, thirst, or sexual desires; finding companionship; asserting oneself; or raising children. If your article idea deals with one of these vital areas, you've selected a topic that will always be interesting and compelling, no matter how much has been written about it previously.

DEVELOP YOUR IDEA ANTENNAE

Once you decide *what* topics interest you, you'll want to know *where* to find them. Actually, good article ideas are everywhere, when you know how to look. I get many of my ideas delivered to my doorstep—in the morning paper. Since most monthly magazines take anywhere from four to twelve months to publish an accepted article, you need to go beyond the headlines or your story will seem stale to editors. Consider the implications of the news: Is there some aspect you've been wondering about that hasn't been covered? What might the headlines imply for the world of tomorrow? Is there a story behind the story that you could cover? A big earthquake, for example, might inspire you to profile one of the scientists who studies quakes, describe the technological innovations in earthquake prediction, or speculate about the future: "Aftershocks—Will Los Angeles Still Be Standing in the 21st Century?"

The smaller stories in the paper can often be more inspiring than the major ones. A three-line item gave me an excellent idea for a medical piece; another filler suggested a good business profile. Classified ads can also be good leads: you might learn of an unusual business or offbeat service to write about. Make a point of clipping and saving these tidbits for future consumption in your work.

Cannibalize the magazine articles you read to build fresh ideas. Your article might take the opposite approach, give in-depth coverage to some intriguing detail the other writer mentions briefly, or use the topic as an example of a larger problem. Nonfiction books can also suggest good article ideas; make a note of any thoughts, reactions, opinions, or feelings generated by your reading matter.

It pays to listen, too. Even a casual conversation with a friend or relative may trigger an idea: what one person likes to talk about could well be something another person would enjoy reading about. A friend's problems could inspire a self-help piece; your spouse's gripes might be the start of a consumer or personal finance topic; your child's recital of her day at school might launch a parenting or education piece.

More money-making ideas may be lurking in the office: look for trade innovations to sell to trade magazines, career strategies for the general interest reader, even relationship ideas. At lectures or conventions, scout around for potential profile subjects and provocative theories or approaches others could benefit from. Use TV and movies to take the pulse of America, looking for current trends and lively lifestyles you could write about.

When you make idea hunting a priority, you'll find yourself collecting ideas faster than you can write them up. Stockpile your ideas against future dry spells by keeping an idea file filled with clippings and notes.

ILLUSTRATION 1-1: Query for Profile Article (Typed on letterhead stationery)

[date]

Ms. Mary Farrell
Senior Associate Editor
Savvy
3 Park Ave.
New York, NY 10016

Dear Ms. Farrell:

I'd like to propose an executive profile of Frances Grill, owner and founder of Click Model Management, a brash young agency (launched in 1980) which *Newsweek* magazine credits with having "almost single-handedly changed the face of modeling in this country."

When other agents were pushing look-alike blondes, Grill created a quirky, imperfect style emphasizing individuality, with such successes as turning 29-year-old Isabella Rossellini, daughter of Ingrid Bergman, into the record holder for an exclusive modeling contract: $2 million over five years from Lancôme Cosmetics.

Grill has overcome tremendous odds to succeed. In a poor Sicilian neighborhood in Brooklyn where Grill was raised, her father used to park his children in a local orphanage when times got tight. After spending many years as a photographer's representative, 58-year-old Grill started her agency with a $100,000 investment, undaunted by the market stranglehold of the Big Four agencies—Ford ($30 million a year in billings), Zoli ($25 million), Wilhelmina ($23 million to $28 million), and Elite ($27 million). From $300,000 in billings the first year, Click now bills $8 million a year. Grill is now venturing into film, as well, with a newly created talent agency, Flick.

I believe this profile would be of great interest to your readers. I'll write it with L. Scott Morgan, who worked with me on a modeling article I just did for *Cosmopolitan*. My writing credits also include *Family Circle, Harper's Magazine, Playgirl, Glamour, Writer's Digest, Publishers Weekly,* and 15 other magazines and newspapers. I've also written a book, *How to Sell Every Magazine Article You Write* (Writer's Digest Books, 1986). I've been a literary agent for the past 12 years, and have taught writing courses at Parson's School of Design.

I'll look forward with interest to your reaction to this exclusive submission.

Sincerely yours,

Lisa Collier Cool

Chapter 2

Secrets of Successful Slanting

If you were a magazine editor, which of these travel queries would you buy: "Vacation Ideas" or "Home Swapping—Your Guide to Free Travel Accommodations"? "Vacation Ideas" is a promising topic, but it's like a shotgun blast: long on coverage, but short on *focus*. "Home Swapping," on the other hand, zeros in on a limited subject with rifle-like precision. It's targeted to sell because it ignites editorial interest with an original and intriguing *slant* on the subject of vacationing.

What is a slant? A slant is more than just a title—the home swapping piece wouldn't lose any of its appeal if you'd chosen some other title for the query, or used no title at all. Instead, it's a way of cutting a big topic that you couldn't describe fully in a book or article into a size that can be explored in detail within the confines of your intended length.

A slant is a center your writing will revolve around. It might be a viewpoint: "The Allure of the Macho, Macho Man"; a theme: "Failure Can Be Good for You"; a narrowly defined subject: "Shopping the Discount Outlets"; a key question: "Are You Being Paid What You're Really Worth?"; an issue: "Combating Teen Suicide"; or even a plan of organization: "The 10-Day Shape-Up Program."

Here's how slanting can save you time and improve your prospects for a sale. Imagine that you've selected politics as the topic for your next piece. Since complete coverage of the subject could easily become your life's work, a few decisions are in order. First, how will you define politics? Is your subject national, state, or city politics; political methods and maneuvers; political opinions; or the exercise of power and strategy in daily life? You might have to repeat the defining process several times to find a subject narrow enough for magazine treatment.

Once you've selected your subcategory, your next question is, "What approach should I use?" You might decide to make the piece sexy, practical, controversial, personality-oriented, humorous, historical, speculative, or descriptive, or you might take any number of other approaches. The end result—your slant—might turn out to be: "The Young and The Restless—The New Wave Reformers," "Winning at Office Politics," "The Art of the Washington Power Lunch," "Your Child Could Be a Congressional Page," or "How Much is That Pork Barrel in the Window?"

THE IMPORTANCE OF SLANT

Since the slant you select will narrow down your submission possibilities, why bother with slanting? The answer is simple: *if you don't have a slant, you don't have a saleable article.* Each magazine specializes in a particular editorial viewpoint, one that addresses the special interests and concerns of a select group of readers. They could be working mothers, senior citizens, computer hackers, any group large enough to justify publication of a specialized magazine. Only through your slant can the editor evaluate whether your article matches its reader profile. "Home Swapping" appeals to the budget-conscious consumer, the target audience of *Family Circle Woman's Day,* and many other publications. "Vacation Ideas," on the other hand, is targeted to everybody—and therefore nobody, in magazine terms.

A strong slant will make for easier sales—and easier writing. By defining your topic clearly before you start writing, you'll reduce research time, frame interviews to provide a maximum of usable quotes, and avoid many of the organizational difficulties that slow writers down. Try writing the "Vacation Ideas" piece, and your research and writing will literally wander all over the map; choose "Home Swapping" and you'll reach your journey's end—the finished piece—with a minimum of unproductive writing detours.

BOOK SLANTS

Slant helps book queries too, by helping editors distinguish between your book idea and other available books on the subject. If your topic is "Motherhood," you'll need to narrow the topic down to find an audience. You might select such slants as "Raising Vegetarian Children," "Pregnancy After 35," "The Working Mother's Resource Book," or "Make Your Own Maternity Wardrobe." Each of these ideas is aimed at a specific kind of reader and is therefore far more saleable than "Motherhood."

However, a book is at least ten times longer than an article, so your book slant should encompass a wider scope than an article slant. If your topic is "Buying a Used Car," your article might cover "The 10 Most Common Used Car Ripoffs," your book *Deals on Wheels—A Complete Guide to Getting Used Car Bargains*. Both have essentially the same angle, saving money on used cars, but they differ in the depth of coverage.

SLANTS THAT SELL

There are two ways to turn a slant into a sale. You can start with a market—perhaps *Parents Magazine* or *Modern Bride*—and tailor your basic idea to its readers—turning "Vacation Ideas" into "What You Should Know About Traveling During Pregnancy" or "Catch the Love Boat with These Honeymoon Cruises." Or you can start with a slant, then look for readers: "Unscrambling the Airfare Maze" and "Luggage that Fits Your Travel Style" are two slants which might appeal to such publications as *Vogue, Travel & Leisure*, or *Parade*.

What's the best slant for your idea? Here are some slants that work for both books and articles:

New!   Novelty can be a slant in itself. If your subject is very new, a basic, informative article is your best bet. A few years ago, I was able to sell several articles on home computers with queries listing statistics attesting to the increasing consumer interest in these high-tech toys. (One of these queries is reproduced on page 44 in chapter 4.) Similarly, such topics as "Windsurfing," "Genetic Counseling," and "Infant Psychiatry" are new enough to sell without elaborate slanting; instead, seduce the editor with juicy facts and provocative quotes.

But what if your subject isn't exactly stop-the-presses news? The favorite trick of the advertising world is to take a familiar product, add a new ingredient or two, change the package, and slap a banner on it proclaiming, "New and Improved!" The same approach works well for familiar article ideas; take a topic like "Infertility Treatments," investigate current research trends and experimental treatments, collect some lively quotes from experts, and title your update query "The Test Tube Baby Boom" or "New Hope for the Infertile."

Sexy Slants.   I'm not talking about keyhole accounts of how the other half loves here, but adding a shot of sex appeal to a piece which is not fundamentally *about* sex. Your financial piece might be enlivened with a brief discussion of the sexy language of stocks: "Short-term investments, often called 'quickies' in the trade. . . ." Or your "Telephone Tactics" query might read, "A sales call must tease the customer along until the climax, the close of the sale." Inserting sexy words and phrases—even a double entendre expression like the one a *Mademoiselle* author used as a title for his piece about growing up male—"Growing Up the Hard Way"—subtly seduces the editors.

A titillating title grabs the reader's eye. A horticulturist I represent enjoyed giant sales on his book on plant propagation, which he titled *Sex in the Garden;* another writer undoubtedly multiplied the readership for his advertising exposé with the title *Subliminal Seduction.* Some other examples: *Your Erroneous Zones*, a self-help book; "Indecent Exposure," a movie industry exposé; *Coffee, Tea or Me?*, the memoirs of an airline stewardess; and *Balls!*, a baseball autobiography.

Money Talks.   Money is another surefire attention getter. Most topics have a money angle; an infertility magazine piece could be slanted as "The Billion-Dollar Baby Quest," giving astounding facts on the high cost of treatments and cures. One of my former clients, Pulitzer Prize winner Fred Sparks, used money to find a unique angle for his Kennedy book: *The Ten-Million Dollar Honeymoon: The Story of Jackie and Ari's First Year.*

Other good money slants are "The Budget Guide to . . ." health clubs, ski vacations, kitchen renovation, you name it; luxury living pieces: "The Best Little Sports Car $100,000 Can Buy"; exposé articles: "Up, Up, and Away—the Hidden Costs of Our Space Program"; celebrity-paycheck articles: "How Much Does Princess Di Cost England?"; salary surveys: "Where the Bucks Are"; and pieces on the spending habits of the super-rich: "A Peek Inside Barbra Streisand's Closet."

Call of the Wild.   Turn an article into an adventure by stimulating the reader's primal impulses. Emphasize danger, survival, life-and-death struggles, predation, and conquest—all themes that readily translate into the modern arena. Make a routine piece about "Corporate Mergers" into a sizzling drama with a title like "Shark Attack!" and query text that describes the new corporate defense arsenal: "poison pills," "golden parachutes," "white knights," "shark repellent," "kamikaze," and "Pac-Man."

Not just for business pieces, the dramatic approach adds fire to queries on sports: "Dance of Death—Should Boxing Be Outlawed?"; medicine: "Stalking the AIDS Virus"; childraising: "The Teenager—Master of Psychological Warfare"; career pieces, "Survive—and Thrive—Under the Tyrannical Boss"; profiles: "The Mouse That Roared"; even travel: "Walking on the Wild Side— Nature Tours."

Psst! Confidential.   There's nothing so fascinating as a secret revealed. Offer editors the inside scoop on your story, using such tell-all titles as "Confessions of a Would-Be Mogul," "An Insider's Stock Picks," "Success Secrets of Executive Women," "An Intimate Look at Those Powerful, Glittering Model Agencies," or "Behind the Scenes at a Broadway Opening." Your inside account could probe the trends in an industry; profile an up-and-coming young success; reveal strategies to increase power, prestige, or profits; or bare scandals or corruption in industry or government.

Where do you find saleable secrets? Your profession is a good starting point: information that may be widely known inside the business could be an eye-opener to those outside it. For example, if you've worked as an interior designer, a good slant on your subject might be "Not for the Trade Only—Secret Decorator Sources You Can Shop, Too." Or find an expert to be your guide; your doctor, lawyer, stockbroker, spouse, or friends could be the "Deep Throat" you cite as a source. (Chapter 6 will tell you how to find authorities to interview.)

Promises, Promises. Motivate editors to buy your piece by promising the reader a specific advantage to be gained from reading your article. Title your investment piece "Smart Ways to Double Your Money", your childrearing article "Games that Raise Baby's IQ", your tax advice "Retire as a Millionaire." Make sure your query substantiates your claims with specifics on how the reader will accomplish these goals: "The average mutual fund doubles an investor's money in eight years, but the high-growth funds I'll recommend have consistently outperformed the average. . . ."

Selling Through Intimidation. Scare tactics can make for an effective slant—if the danger you warn of is a genuine problem and you have a program of action to help the reader cope. When offering her medical piece to *Mademoiselle*, a writer I know used the title "Protect Your Fertility." Naturally, the young, single readers of this publication would be concerned about any possible threat to future reproduction, and were therefore the ideal audience for this cautionary advice. A more extreme approach worked for another writer; he titled his AIDS article "Slow-Motion Death" and quoted horrifying scientific projections about the spread of this deadly disorder. *Penthouse* promptly commissioned the piece.

The threat need not be medical; your query could address such concerns as "Is Your Child Using Drugs?"; "Date Rape"; "Fire! Are You Prepared?"; or "Detecting the Dishonest Job Applicant."

Unexpected Reversals. Turnabout is fair play—and a good sales strategy. Frequently all you need to do to create an original slant is to present the opposite viewpoint to the issue. If the conventional wisdom is that unstructured classes increase children's creativity, your piece might make a case for the other side: "Bring Back the Three R's." The illustration on page 23 contains one of my queries that took a contrary position successfully.

One of my clients, Harry Browne, offered an unorthodox economic approach in his book *You Can Profit from a Monetary Crisis*, which was a No. 1 best-seller for many months. Browne attributes his success to his appeal to a minority—those who believed that gold, silver, and foreign currencies were better investments in the early 1970s than stocks. A minority, Browne believes, is starved for confirmation of its ideas and thus is highly motivated to read the work of those who also hear a different drummer.

Betting on the Numbers.   Ever notice how many books and articles have a number or two in their titles? Numbers can make a good organizing principle for pieces that are essentially collections of some sort: "The 50 Best Doctors in the United States," "Ten Ways to Slash Mortgage Costs," "Twenty-five Plants You Can Grow in the Shade," "Five Women Who Risked It All—and Won."

Time can be a good slant as well: "A Day in the Life of . . .," "Ten Days to Super Sex," "Thin Thighs in 30 Days." Dates give your query an up-to-the-minute ring, too: "Romance in the '80s" or "Smart Money Guide for 1988" sound like they contain the latest information and trends. Or fit your idea into a time capsule by connecting the past and present into a nostalgia piece—"Woodstock Revisited"—or projecting into the future—"2001: A Futuristic Sexual Odyssey."

Mapping Out a Slant.   Geography can be a good slant. For city and regional publications, look for the local angle: "When the Chips Are Down: Why the Computer Boom Turned Out to Be Another Texan Tall Tale," "The Radon Fallout in New Jersey," "Making Book in New York: Untold Tales from Publisher's Row." Or make several regional articles out of the same idea: "A Brownstone Grows in Brooklyn," "Urban Homesteading in Chicago's Brownstones," and "Renovating the Boston Brownstone."

For national magazines, use location more broadly. Use the events in a particular city or town as a model, cautionary lesson, or inspiration to all of us: "Safe Rides: How One Town Sobered Up the Drunk Drivers for Life," "The Healing Waters—When the Dam Burst, Town and Gown Stood Together Again," or "The Moonshine Wars—An Adventure in Law Enforcement." You can also use location in the abstract: "Sex in the Executive Suite," "Finding the Right Adult Education Program," "Elevator Etiquette," "Setting up the Home Office."

Have Slant, Will Travel.   For travel articles, the more extensively your territory has been covered, the sharper your slant must be. For destinations inside the United States, thinking in terms of a family trip can be a good approach: "Seeing Colonial Williamsburg through a Child's Eyes," "Camping along the Appalachian Trail," "Ski Resorts With Child Care Facilities," "Vacationing with Pets." Other possibilities are unusual tours: "Discovering Black America,"

"White Water Rafting," "Teen Cycle Trips," "Riverboating down the Mississippi"; lesser-known locations: "The Amish Country"; and budget travel: "D.C. on $25 a Day."

For familiar European cities, try "The Hidden Rome" or "Excavating the Louvre," which can discuss the fascinating sights to be seen *underground* in these cities. Tell the reader about exciting sidetrips—"Visiting Delphi" and annual festivals—"Running with the Bulls." Describe unusual hotels, nude beaches, where to find the best bargains, and memorable dining. For hobbyist and sports magazines, you could cover such topics as "Windsurfing in Greece" or "Italian Lace Making."

Tickling the Funny Bone.   If your approach amuses an editor, you may find yourself laughing all the way to the bank when your piece is commissioned. Though a humorous slant wouldn't be appropriate for every topic, it can liven up a surprising variety of subjects. For women's magazines, follow in the footsteps of Erma Bombeck and Jean Kerr with a lighthearted slant on such subjects as housekeeping: "Single White Sock Seeks Mate"; pets: "How I Used Up Eight of My Lives Raising Kittens"; and children: "All Right, Who Hid the Refrigerator?" Or take a sexier, more sophisticated approach for publications like *Glamour:* "For Sale: One Lover, Slightly Used."

Other good topics for humor are fashion; business: "Fail Your Way to the Top"; consumerism; sports: "The Wooden Glove Awards"; politics: "Ten Surefire Ways to Resurrect a Dead Voter"; lifestyles and current trends; medicine; and travel: "The Vacation that Will Live in Infamy."

Gee Whiz!   A good slant for scientific, futuristic, medical, or technological writing, this approach is designed to elicit amazement or wonder from the reader: "Gee whiz, that's incredible!" Compiling and interpreting surprising facts are the keys to this angle; for example, in your book query on pheromones (sex attractant chemicals) you might say, "Human pheromones may explain such diverse phenomena as love at first sight and serial murders, according to recent studies by. . . ."

The gee-whiz slant can provoke horror or outrage: your query might document some of medicine's worst blunders, examples of monumental stupidity in government officials or business leaders, flagrant miscarriages of justice, shoddy or hazardous manufacturing procedures, or other exposé topics.

The Best.   A good way to jazz up profiles or other article topics is through *positioning,* an advertising technique that sells products—like your article queries—by creating unique slots for them in the marketplace. Use superlatives to establish your position: "America's Richest Women," "Ghosts in New York's Oldest Cathedral," "The Smallest Babies—New Hope for the Premature," "The Best Brownies in Baltimore." "First" and "last" are also strong positions.

A position can also be created through reflected glory; connect your article idea to acknowledged masters or celebrities, and some of their cachet will rub off on your piece. Do this through the title—"Machiavellian Maneuvers: Unorthodox Routes to Success"—or with celebrity references in the body of the query: "Brigitte Bardot tried to end her life on the 40th anniversary of the day she began it. For some, a birthday can be a traumatic event, but my article, 'Beating the Birthday Blues,' will supply expert advice on aging gracefully—and happily."

TITLE TIPS

Selecting titles is the least important aspect of selling your article, because most magazines will change the title when the piece is published. However, a good title can still have a positive effect, so it's worth devoting a few minutes' thought to it. Your title should reflect both the slant and the tone of the article; don't use a lighthearted title on a query for a serious article.

Good titles can come from a variety of sources, such as famous quotations or partial quotations: "Old Wine in New Bottles" was a title I used for a *Writer's Digest* piece on selling recycled article ideas; puns and plays on words: "Replaceable You" was the title of a piece on artificial body parts; provocative questions: "Is Your Spouse Having an Affair?"; colorful phrases from your piece: "Night of the Hackers"; new words you've coined: "Drownproofing" was the title of a piece in *People* magazine; statistics and numbers: "Triple Your Reading Speed"; action-oriented statements: "Revamp Your Office Image"; and commands: "Stop, Thief!"

What if you can't think of a good title? Rather than omit the title,

ILLUSTRATION 2-1: The Unexpected Reversal

July 7, 1983

Mr. William Brohaugh
Editor
Writer's Digest
9933 Alliance Rd.
Cincinnati, OH 45242

Dear Mr. Brohaugh:

I'd like to propose an article idea: "Old Wine in New Bottles." As a literary agent and writing teacher, I have found that a common problem among starting magazine writers is a lack of inspiration. Every idea seems to have been done, and yet the magazines come out month after month with articles that make the would-be writer say, "I could have thought of that!" In my own experience as a professional writer and in that of my many successful clients, the real problem is *not* a lack of inspiration.

Inspiration is not necessary—or even desirable—in selling articles. Instead, the secret is to take commonplace and familiar subjects and give them a slightly new twist. For example, coping with rejection is a topic that is discussed regularly in women's magazines, and yet one of my clients recently sold it to *Cosmopolitan.* Popularity is another staple of teen publications, yet another client landed an assignment from *Seventeen* to cover it. Home computers have had millions of words devoted to them, but I have sold *four* separate articles on the subject (to *Gallery, Club, Cosmopolitan,* and the North American Newspaper Alliance).

Selling unoriginal ideas is a matter of timing. Many magazines tend to cover the same subjects every three or four years. If they haven't done it lately (or have it in the works), they might buy it from *you.* In the article (which will contain quotes from magazine editors), I will show the reader how to identify such potentially saleable topics, provide ways to think of new approaches to old subjects, and offer suggestions on marketing such queries. I think this article would be a refreshing change from the usual advice, which gives the impression that you need imagination to sell.

What do you think? I will also cover how to sell the same unoriginal idea over and over. (In addition to the home computer idea, I have several other ideas I managed to sell two or three times, using different approaches). [I then described my background briefly here.]

Sincerely yours,

Lisa Collier Cool

Since many writers think editors want only original article ideas, I took the opposite tack in this query, which sold to *Writer's Digest.*

just slap on a working title which sums up the subject in a few words: "Foreign Exchange Traders." Or try a standard title, such as "How to . . .," "What You Should Know About . . .," or "The Truth About. . . ." If your subject is interesting, a bland title won't detract from your query; it's really the text of the query that makes or breaks the sale.

Chapter 3

Leads That Hook the Editor

What's the best way to get an editor's attention? "Punch him in the nose," says one of my best-selling clients, summing up the purpose of a good first paragraph. Your opener—or *lead*—must pack a powerful wallop, or you may lose the sales fight in the first round. The right lead will not only capture and hold a busy editor's interest, but it will vividly introduce your topic and slant. With this tantalizing display of your writing style, you'll stimulate a desire to buy your piece.

The time invested in creating a winning lead can pay off doubly: first, use the lead to entice the editor to buy; then, once you've sold the piece, use the same lead to launch the article or book. Much of your query can be recycled; the summary techniques described in chapter 4 often yield lively subheads and openings to paragraphs within the body of the piece. And a good biography (described in chapter 5) can be easily adapted to future queries.

To judge whether the lead you select is effective, try the "bar test." Here's how writer Carl Bakal describes it in *A Treasury of Tips for Writers*, edited by Marvin Weisbord: "Imagine yourself in a bar wanting to strike up a conversation with a fellow tippler. Would the lead you have in mind provoke his curiosity, get him to want to know more about the subject you are talking—or writing—about?" Another journalist, Edward Brecher, also quoted in *A Treasury of Tips for Writers*, illustrates the "bar test" in action with this real-life snippet of bar dialogue he overheard: "What a day! I've just finished performing an autopsy on a 316-pound, 16-year-old female gorilla!" Makes you wonder what the speaker said next, doesn't it? That's the true test of a successful lead: it compels the reader to move to the *next* paragraph.

THE FIVE Ws—THE FOUNDATION OF A LEAD

How do you start constructing a lead? Glance at the first paragraph of a few newspaper stories, and you'll see a formula. Let's dissect a typical example, a lead I wrote for the *Westsider*, a New York weekly newspaper: "This fall will be a season of paradox at Parsons School of Design. America's oldest interior design program, the department of Environmental Design, will be headed by one of America's most avant-garde and contemporary designers, James Wines."

It has five components:

- *When?* "This fall."
- *Where?* "Parsons School of Design." (Since this is a New York paper, I've omitted the information that Parsons is located in New York City.)
- *What?* "America's oldest interior design program, the department of Environmental Design," has a new chairman.
- *Who?* ". . . one of America's most avant-garde and contemporary designers, James Wines."
- *Why?* By using the phrase "season of paradox" in the first sentence, I've created a question in the reader's mind: Why will this fall be a season of paradox at Parsons? The second sentence answers it by explaining that "America's oldest interior design program . . . will be headed by one of America's most avant-garde and contemporary designers. . . ." Naturally, this in turn poses the question of *why* this designer was selected, which moves the reader into the rest of the profile, where I satisfy curiosity with facts about Wines and his plans for Parsons.

While the basic five Ws lead can lack flash and fire—and therefore is best used on newsy magazine stories—it's a good starting point to producing a lead for any query. Each W helps you identify key ingredients of your story. Ask yourself, *where* and *when* does the action take place? and you might find yourself writing, "Backwater,

Missouri, population 210, was just another sleepy village until the residents woke up America with a $500 million lawsuit last July."

Even if the first two Ws don't figure in your piece, the questions of *who*, *what*, and *why* certainly should: "For the severely obese, an inflatable balloon placed in the stomach may be the best way to curb overeating, say researchers at ABC Hospital, whose patients have lost an average of 103 pounds each after the device was implanted."

THE INVERTED PYRAMID

A second newspaper formula, the *inverted pyramid*, is another valuable aid in structuring your lead—and the paragraphs that follow. The idea behind the inverted pyramid is simple: *lead with your strongest material, save the details for later.* Avoid using the first paragraph to warm up, as some inexperienced writers do; the editor's interest may have cooled by the time your prose heats up. Instead shoot first, answer questions later. Here's how to organize your opening paragraphs:

Arouse Interest.   "How would you like to double your savings?" "When Jeanette Berdona went into labor shortly before 4 A.M., she had no idea she was about to make medical history." "Watch out manufacturers—building a better mousetrap might just be the route to bankruptcy."

Next, Provide Specifics.   "When a small air purifier company received hundreds of unsolicited testimonials asserting that its product was a miracle cure for many respiratory disorders, the company thought it had struck it rich. Large ads reproduced these comments, and the checks poured in—along with a stream of demands from the Food and Drug Administration for clinical studies and tests. Though no harmful effect of the device was ever discovered, the cost of complying with FDA regulations forced the company into receivership."

Close With Your Key Point.   "Is it a crime to sell a safe, effective product to the American consumer? My cautionary tale, 'When the Watchdog Goes Mad,' will chronicle how one small business was regulated right out of existence merely for doing its job *too* well, ex-

posing the urgent need for a system of checks and balances to control the excesses of the FDA."

Once you've established your priorities, you're ready to start
writing the lead. Remember, there are no hard and fast rules as to
what kind of lead will work best for *your* query; an effective lead can
be one sentence or a few paragraphs, an elaborate description or a
plain recitation of facts, a traditional formula or a unique approach
of your own devising. And any of these leads is equally appropriate
for either book or article queries.

THE ARTFUL ANECDOTE

An old favorite that never goes out of style is the anecdotal lead. It's
a one-two punch: first you *show* the reader the problem or situation
with an illustrative case history or two, then you *tell* the story behind the story, giving chapter and verse on the main point of the article or book with appropriate facts and figures.

An effective anecdote provokes a reaction and gets the reader
involved in the story. You can produce shock by opening your query
on bicycle safety with a horrifying description of youthful bicyclists
weaving recklessly down a congested street; amusement with a
lighthearted recollection of your dating mishaps; sadness with your
recounting of a friend's miscarriage; surprise with a story about
mountaineers who turn out to be ascending in wheelchairs; or outrage with a portrayal of judicial misconduct.

For many queries, a success story can be a good opening, since
it quickly alerts the editor to the benefits readers can gain from reading your piece. Here's how I used this approach to sell an article
called "The Gold Mine in Gothic Novels":

> Max Barrett sold his first gothic novel to Berkley Books
> for $3,500. A four-book contract with the same publisher
> quickly followed, and now—$30,000 later—he's at work
> on his sixth book. "I wasn't sure what to do with my
> life," says Barrett. "I was just knocking around from one
> job to another, and I wrote my first gothic as something
> of a lark. I never dreamed it would sell."
>
> A new gothic is published every day in the United
> States, and experts estimate that they earn their authors

more than $2 million annually. An early example, *Rebecca*, by Daphne du Maurier, has become one of the best-selling books of all time with approximately three million copies in hardcover, while gothic novelists Victoria Holt and Phyllis A. Whitney are now millionaires. Dozens more make yearly incomes of $25,000 to $75,000. Still, although the gothic market is quite receptive to newcomers, many beginning writers are unaware of this high-paying outlet.

Illustrating the pitfalls you'll help the reader avoid can be just as effective as an opening, as long as your next paragraph makes it clear that you'll supply the solution to the problem. Whether your anecdote accentuates the positive or warns of negative consequences, it's important to match the characters in your example to the intended readership of the article. If your query is targeted to *Savvy*, for example, the incident you relate should focus on an upwardly mobile, executive woman. Readers will then *identify* with the story.

Dropping the names of celebrities or prominent individuals in your anecdote is another attention-getting device, especially if the luminary you select offers a spectacular example of your subject matter:

> A taste for danger, once acquired, can be extraordinarily seductive for the confirmed risk-taker. Novelist Graham Greene, who missed death by one click of the revolver's chamber, described his experiment with Russian roulette as being "like a young man's first successful experience of sex."

OTHER PUNCHY LEADS

Still stuck for a good opening? Here is a variety of other approaches to try:

A Question. Here's how Amy Sunshine-Genova opened a query that produced a $750 sale to *Cosmopolitan*:

> "He's perfect," my friend Ellie confided to my answering

machine. "Nice-looking, clever, a cardiac surgeon—and he wants to take me to dinner. What's wrong with this picture?" (For the full text of this query, see the illustration on page 34.)

Facts.   Cramming your lead with specifics is a good way to convince the editor of your expertise. Your presentation can be plain or fancy, as long as it has plenty of numbers, dollar signs, and other particulars. Here's how I opened a piece on "Writing for Confession Magazines":

> Confession is good for the soul—and the bank balance. Last year, confession magazines paid out nearly $1 million for new stories. At the current rate of 3 to 5 cents a word, this works out to $150 to $250 per story—money that could soon be accruing in your savings account once you understand the simple formula used in this type of writing.

In the next lead, I combined the anecdotal and factual approaches to set the scene for an article on modeling:

> 11:30 A. M. Outside Click Model Management, the Kimberlys, Jennifers, and Ericas clutch snapshots or portfolios, hoping to break into New York's $150 million modeling business, where a beautiful 15-year-old can earn $3,000—or more—for a day's work. It's the monthly "open call," where anyone who thinks she's got the right stuff can audition with Click booker Bonnie Tayar. Precisely at noon, Bonnie steps out into the crowded hallway, announcing, "Anyone under 5'8", please go home." Two girls slink off.

Quotes and Dialogue.   Using quotes or dialogue can add color and drama to your material, as well as allow you to make points that would be difficult to present effectively in the third person. Your speaker can be an expert, prominent figure or simply a person with first-hand experience of the subject, as in this lead I wrote for a *Playgirl* piece on "Romance in the '80s":

"Frankly, I'm desperate," says Shelley Kusnetz, a 34-year-old, unmarried photographer. "I'm convinced that single women are cloning themselves, while unattached men are vanishing into thin air. I'm not looking for Mr. Perfect, just a bright, witty man in his 30s. While I have an active social life, I'm beginning to hate dating—especially first dates. What I want is a relationship, or possibly marriage. I feel that I have plenty to offer the right man—I'm reasonably attractive, fairly successful, and have a warm, friendly personality. So where is he?"

Shelley is far from alone in her search for that "significant other". . . .

Comparisons and contrasts.   "Novelty stores used to sell cans of air as gag gifts. Today, it's food manufacturers who are attempting to sell air, in the form of 'slack fill,' an industry phrase for the increasingly common practice of selling food in half-empty packages designed to deceive the consumer into thinking he's getting more for his money than he actually is."

Uncommon Leads.   Some less frequently used but still potentially powerful openings are witty definitions, commands to the reader, surprising twists, and shockers: "While the Smith family was hurtling down the roller coaster, their dog, left in the car while the family visited Disney World, was slowly dying as the temperature inside the locked car soared to 150 degrees."

LEADS GOING NOWHERE

Though the touch of an expert writer can bring any lead to life, certain leads can be hazardous to the saleability of your query—and therefore should be avoided when you're starting out.

Consider this lackluster lead: "What do Mark Twain, Anaïs Nin, Walt Whitman, Edgar Allan Poe, and Carl Sandburg have in common? All of these famous writers have self-published their work, as have Virginia Woolf, D. H. Lawrence, and Edgar Rice Burroughs."

While questions often produce lively first sentences, this extended list arouses only the mildest curiosity in the reader. The second sentence has an even greater flaw—it completely satisfies whatever slight interest the preceding one has produced, leaving the reader no strong reason to read on.

A better approach would be to appeal to the reader's self-interest with an opening that clearly demonstrates how he or she personally can benefit from your proposed article: "Self-publishing is pleasing to your vanity—and your pocketbook. While the typical hardcover publisher gives you a mere 10 percent of the price of your book, publishing it yourself allows you to collect 100 percent of the profits—and have complete editorial control of your work. This surprisingly affordable alternative. . . ."

Other leads on the editorial "least wanted" list include feeble jokes and bad puns; dictionary definitions (invent your own); quickly dated references (remember, it may be a year before the article you sell sees print); lengthy geographical descriptions (start with action); highly technical material or jargon (save the nuts and bolts for later in the article); excessive scene setting or historical background (editors call this "throat clearing"); and claims not substantiated by later text.

MORE POWERFUL PROSE

Once you've roughed out a tentative lead, add some sparkle to your style and approach. Here's a quick editorial checklist that will help you strengthen your writing:

• Have you created interest in your query subject, establishing right up front what your subject is (for easy referral by an editor), using a style and tone appropriate to your overall subject?

• Is the writing vivid and the sentence structure varied? Mark Twain once observed that the difference between the correct word and the nearly correct word is "the difference between lightning and the lightning bug." The arrangement of those words is equally vital; though the average sentence is about fourteen words long, for snappier writing use a combination of long and short sentences to create more interesting rhythms.

• Could it be shortened? Often, cutting a few unnecessary words or phrases will greatly improve your prose. Imagine the lead is a telegram you're sending out for a dollar a word; are you getting your money's worth out of each word? Alert yourself to space-wasting introductory phrases: "At this point in time"; use of passive constructions: change "a book which is published directly by its author . . ." to "a self-published book . . ." ; and over-reliance on adjectives rather than action verbs: "the train entered the station slowly" would sound better as "the train crawled into the station."

• Is it specific and factual? Editors are quick to sense when a writer is hedging. Don't say, "Twin pregnancy is relatively rare"; write, "One out of 90 pregnancies results in a twin birth; one out of 10,000 produces triplets." Use details: instead of saying "gun," for example, put "Smith and Wesson .38 special."

• Have you eliminated most clichés? Such pat phrases as "rich as Croesus," "sweet as pie," and "dog-tired" have lost all meaning through overuse. While an occasional cliché is acceptable, instead of writing "she was pretty as a picture," try for an original description, like "She didn't have a drop-dead beauty, but rather a subtle sensuality that drew your eye to her face again and again." Or use the familiar phrase in a new context to add a lively dimension to your work: "Looking like a million helps, but to *make* a million a model must . . ."

• Does the last sentence of your lead compel the reader to continue? If not, revise until it does.

Don't fall in love with your initial effort, as many inexperienced writers do. Remembering the importance of making a powerful, positive first impression, experiment with different styles and approaches for your opening until you find one that resonates with unmistakable meaning and purpose. *Then* you have a lead that works.

ILLUSTRATION 3-1

What's Wrong with This Picture?

Why We Get Nervous When Things Seem Too Good

by

Amy Sunshine-Genova

"He's perfect," my friend Ellie confided to my answering machine. "Nice-looking, clever, a cardiac surgeon—and he wants to take me to dinner. What's wrong with this picture?"

Nothing much, it turns out. Ellie's been dating the guy happily for six months now, his only serious flaw being "the nagging feeling I get that things are too good. I'm waiting for the bubble to burst."

Who among us has never gotten the jitters when things go well? And why is it so easy for that familiar tug of worry to interfere with our good times?

"Fear of happiness is pervasive," explains Dr. Milton Shumsky, a clinical psychologist. "We're taught from an early age to knock wood when we acknowledge something good. The Italians call it *malocchio,* the Jews know it as *kineahora,* but the concept is the same: the evil eye, a jealous god, will get you if you're too happy. The only means of protection, it follows, is to diminish your enjoyment."

My own grandmother, who took this lesson to heart, made a profession of dampening enthusiasm. "Don't get your hopes up," she'd admonish, "and you won't be disappointed."

Another woman I know traces her fear of happiness to her childhood viewing of *The Wizard of Oz.* "Every time the munchkins celebrated," she recalls, "the wicked witch would descend. I figured that having fun left you much too vulnerable."

Some of us sabotage our happiness more vividly than others. My friend Jean twisted her ankle two days after receiving a well-deserved promotion, and the same week, cut her hand. "I'm not normally accident-prone," she insists. "I really think I brought the injuries on myself. I'd been feeling guilty all week, like somehow this new position would make life too easy."

Jean's guilt isn't unusual, according to Dr. Shumsky. "If you grow up believing on some level that suffering is a virtue and happiness is dangerous, you're likely to feel uncomfortable with success. In its more serious forms, self-sabotage can lead to an inappropriate choice of mates or jobs, or keep you from exploring your higher potential."

How can we avert this fate? The answer lies in learning to recognize our fear of happiness and how it operates in our lives. Armed with this awareness, experts say, we can short-circuit our anxieties and live more fully.

I'm an account executive for a top New York public relations firm, with 10 years of professional writing experience in psychology and health. My work has been published in the *Los Angeles Times*, the *Dallas Times-Herald*, *Nation's Business*, and many other publications nationwide. I've been a professional mental health counselor at a community guidance clinic and director of public information for the Mental Health Association.

This is a good story, knock wood, and I look forward to your reply.

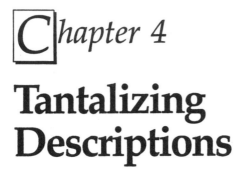

Chapter 4

Tantalizing Descriptions

With an enticing lead, you whet the editor's interest in your proposed piece. To create a hunger to buy, however, you need some meatier fare to present—an enticing description of the major ingredients of the article. Your summary should be deliciously succinct, yet filled with appetizing bits of information. Sprinkle it with some persuasive sales points, and you'll have a recipe for writing sales.

What kind of material should you include in your summary? While the best points to highlight vary according to the subject you select for your book or article, most summaries will include some of these elements:

Statement of Purpose. If you haven't made your subject and slant crystal clear in your lead, make sure this information appears early in your summary, preferably in the first paragraph of this section. Here's how: "My book will be a complete guide to subchapter S incorporation," or "The article will focus on female daredevils and what compels them to deliberately seek out danger."

Outline. Once the editor understands *what* you plan to write about, he or she will want to know *how* you plan to cover the topic. Select anywhere from three to six interesting topics that you'll be discussing, and devote a few sentences to each. Avoid school outlines with roman numerals and capital letters—these are both dull and unprofessional. Instead write something like this:

> • The bottom line—tips on doing a complete credit check on a prospective business partner, as well as ways to gauge the success of any ventures he's currently associated with.

Facts and Figures. There's no better way to prove you have a good story than to cite some relevant facts or statistics as evidence. Though it takes a bit of extra effort to turn "Most of us don't really get our money's worth from the food we buy" into "The typical shopper wastes 20 cents out of each grocery dollar on food she'll end up throwing away," investing a bit of your time in research can really pay off. Editors are put off by vague generalities, perceiving them as signs of laziness in the author; specifics show the editor that you've done your homework.

The illustration on page 44 contains a query that uses many facts to persuade the editor to buy. The article sold to a men's magazine for $750.

Remember, however, that you can have *too* much of a good thing. Encyclopedic recitations of information can be dry and unexciting, as well as time-consuming to compile. (Chapter 6 will describe easy ways to get information quickly.) Instead, look for nuggets that will serve as sales ammunition: "Since one out of three Americans—a total of almost 70 million—is at risk for an accidental injury in the next 12 months, my book on accident prevention could help prevent some of these needless tragedies by alerting readers to potential hazards in their environment." Facts can also add drama to your description: "Fifty percent of all automobile-related injuries occur because the victim has neglected one simple precaution: buckling his seat belt."

Sources. If you're an inexperienced writer, you'll find that your biggest hurdle is establishing your credibility with editors, who may be wondering if they should risk their assignment dollars on an unknown. You can easily overcome this difficulty by mentioning the names of some respected experts you plan to interview for the piece: "Ruth Berini, director of the National Genetics Foundation, and

Lawrence Shapiro, M.D., director of medical genetics at Westchester County Medical Center, have offered me their cooperation in compiling my piece on 'Genetic Counseling.' " (To find the right experts for your piece, consult chapter 6 for tips.)

While it's always best to mention at least one expert by name, if you haven't located your experts yet, you could discuss the *type* of expert you'll be talking to: "My suggestions on 'Getting Promoted' will be drawn from interviews with executive women, personnel managers, and career counselors." Don't list the books or articles you'll consult, unless you have access to extremely exclusive material not available to other journalists: "The confidential memos my source has given me (sample attached) will expose a widespread pattern of corruption in the XYZ industry."

Case Histories. Anecdotes and examples are just as effective in your summary as in your lead. Use them to illustrate key points: "Stuntmen and women can collect some very healthy paychecks for risking life and limb—Dan Johnson once collected $150,000 for six *seconds* of work. To collect that stratospheric salary, he donned a business suit and jumped off the roof of a Toronto skyscraper. One hundred or so stories (1,150 feet) later, he opened his parachute and floated the remaining 300 feet to safety."

Quotes. If you've already interviewed one or more of your experts or are proposing a profile piece, a vivid quote or two can add power to your summary: "The neonatal intensive care unit nurses find their work emotionally wrenching, reports Juliana Fitzhughes of ABC Hospital: 'We all cried when Baby Miller died. After her mother abandoned her, the mothers of several of our patients gave their own milk to help her survive. She rallied briefly, but she was just too small and too sick.' "

Quotes also create a sense of authority. It's one thing for you, a new writer, to claim that hypnosis will help the reader shed those surplus pounds, and another for the same claim to be presented in a quote from Barbara DeBetz, M.D., a psychiatrist specializing in hypnosis, who has just published a book on the topic. For human interest stories, quote one of the participants to add immediacy, color, and drama to your description; for exposés, shock the editor with a powerful indictment direct from the lips of someone in the position to know the facts.

Nuts and Bolts. Though not all writers include this information, you may want to mention the proposed length of your article in words, rounded off to the nearest 500. (For books, round off the word count to the nearest 5,000). The typical length of short articles is between 1,000 and 2,000 words; for medium-length articles, it's 2,500 to 3,500 words; and for long articles, 4,000 to 6,000. (If your proposed piece is less than 1,000 words, don't use a query—just write the article and submit it.) A few magazines buy articles of more than 6,000 words. Check writers' directories, the writer's guidelines the magazine offers, or recent issues of the publication to learn what length the magazine prefers.

For some articles or books, your intended format might be of interest. For example, if you're writing about "Telecommunications Jobs," your query might state, "Each job category will include a description of the job, the average and starting salaries, education and other training required, working conditions, and future prospects for the field."

Themes. For articles that are more philosophical than practical or factual, such as self-help pieces or inspirational subjects, your summary might focus on important messages the reader will find in the piece: "Quiet acts of courage, triumphs of the spirit rather than the flesh, lack the flash and fire of setting another *Guinness Book* record but often require greater daring and always lead to more profound inner growth."

Background/Future. The significance of your subject may sometimes be best understood in the context of the past or future. If, for example, you were pitching a piece on home computers, you might write:

> A computer that would have cost $1 million in 1946 costs less than $1,000 today. . . . The computer of 1946 filled several rooms, used enough electricity to power a small apartment building, and required around-the-clock maintenance. Today's computer fits on a desktop, uses no more electricity than a light bulb, and needs little maintenance. A comparable improvement in the automobile would have us driving Rolls Royces that get three million miles to the gallon and sell for $1.50.

(The full text of this query appears in the illustration on page 44.)

In profile queries, a brief biographical sketch of your subject is essential; if it seems likely that he or she is headed toward a major future achievement, you'll also want to emphasize future prospects along with past accomplishments.

Predictions that the article topic you've chosen will be even more important in the future are a strong selling point for any article. Naturally these claims should be accompanied by some compelling evidence: "Computer jobs are the No. 1 growth field for the '80s, according to U.S. Department of Labor figures. Other experts expect to see 33 percent of all jobs involve computer use by the year 2000." Such arguments offer the editor a powerful motive to buy your "Computer Jobs" article.

Relevance to Reader. If you're sending a query on "Shopping for Your Layette" to *American Baby Magazine,* it's easy enough for an editor to see why your article would interest their readership of expectant and new mothers. You need not state the obvious by pointing out the appeal of this piece to this readership. However, if the relevance of your piece to a particular publication's reader is less than apparent at first glance, include an appropriate explanation in your summary.

Let's say you've decided to send your piece on "Office Politics" to *Parents Magazine.* Why should the editor buy it? Motivate her by pointing out (1) that the office relationships you'll be discussing closely parallel family relationships, with the boss as parent and workers as rival siblings—a good selling point since this magazine emphasizes family concerns; and (2) that the many working mothers in *Parents'* readership can learn how to use their parenting skills to advantage in the office. Such subtle marketing factors are worth exploring; use them to multiply the possible markets for your work.

Timing Tie-Ins. Everyone knows when Christmas is, but how many editors will realize that your Sherlock Holmes piece could be bought and published to coincide with a significant, upcoming anniversary of some milestone in Arthur Conan Doyle's career? If you have good reason to anticipate an upsurge of interest in your topic eight to twelve months after your anticipated delivery date—the typical lead time for most monthly magazines is six to twelve months—explain the timing considerations in your summary:

"Since both Bantam and Simon & Schuster have books on the subject scheduled for September release, with major advertising and promotion, I expect considerable public debate on the topic this fall. If my article were published in August, we could capitalize on this excitement."

Your topic need not be earth-shaking to benefit from this approach. I recently read about a woman who once successfully marketed a light humor piece about a grade school election by suggesting that it would provide an amusing counterpoint to the more serious coverage likely to ensue from the upcoming Presidential elections. A good reason to publish in some particular month can translate into a motivation to publish a piece the editor might not otherwise buy at all.

News Pegs. Current events can be another good marketing tool. Look for media coverage of your topic, and cite it as further evidence of the potential need for your article: "Perhaps you saw the recent *People Weekly* story on Ms. Superfamous Celebrity's 10-year battle with this problem. Although a cure is not yet at hand, the new research findings I'll be discussing suggest several treatment options that did not exist when Ms. Celebrity was first afflicted, offering new hope to thousands of other victims of this painful disorder."

Just about any reportage on your subject can be helpful; mention recent survey findings, medical discoveries, major or minor news stories, radio or TV coverage, celebrity connections, articles in scientific or medical journals, even extensive local coverage if you're offering a human interest, true crime, or real-life drama in your query. The only kind of media coverage that isn't a good sales point is stories in publications *similar* to the one you're trying to sell to—*Glamour* doesn't want to duplicate *Mademoiselle*'s articles.

Illustrations (Optional). If you have a knack for photography or drawing, you can sometimes pick up an extra fee by selling pictures along with your words. Describe the type of illustration you can provide—pen and ink sketches, charts or diagrams, black and white photos, color transparencies—and exactly what the illustrations will depict: "To illustrate the book, I can supply color photos of these zoo veterinarians making their rounds, which in a typical day might cover everything from examining a boa constrictor to extracting an infected tooth from a lion."

To demonstrate your professional skills, submit a few sample illustrations of the type you plan to use for the article. If you're proposing to supply black and white photos of your profile subject, for example, one or two photographic portraits you've done previously of other subjects would be appropriate samples. Be sure your name, address, and phone number appear on the back of the illustration or on the frame of color transparencies. Published illustrations are preferable to unpublished work as samples; send photocopies or tear sheets of the published pictures, mentioning the name of the publication and date of appearance.

If illustration isn't your forte, you may still be able to pick up extra fees for pictures. I've frequently had people I was planning to write about offer to supply pictures. Always check with your interviewees and any organizations you contact as to availability of photos. (Also ask organizations for a press kit; these often have both pictures and helpful facts you could include in your query.) Manufacturers, press agents, hospitals, tourist bureaus, and chambers of commerce are also potential picture sources. For additional ideas on free photos, consult *Picture Sources* (Special Libraries Association) and other photographic reference books.

If you don't plan to provide pictures, you still may want to offer any ideas you have on illustration to help the editor visualize the article more clearly. While you should avoid pointing out the obvious—editors can find pictures of Athens to illustrate your travel piece easily enough—more original suggestions are worth including: "The *Standard Star* ran a number of photos of the victim, as well as a number of shots of the defendant in his various disguises. You might want to buy the rights to these pictures to illustrate my piece."

For further ideas on profiting from your photos, consult *Sell and Resell Your Photos*, by Rohn Engh, an excellent guide to the subject.

Extras. Along with your basic article, you may wish to offer the editor a quiz, sidebar (short, related article), or one or more boxes (supershort, related items such as a list of names and addresses to contact for further information). If, for example, your proposed article discusses "Protecting Your Home from Burglars," a suitable box would be "Crime Facts," where you list various surprising statistics on the incidence of crime in the United States. Most editors like these short items because they add a lively new dimension to the piece and allow for a more interesting graphic approach.

WINNOWING OUT THE CHAFF

If this summary menu proves *too* inspiring and you find yourself with more than one and a half double-spaced, typed pages of descriptive material, your query may be overly long. While the importance of your subject is the best guide to length, queries of two double-spaced pages or less are preferable for most submissions.

If length is a problem, use judicious pruning to reduce your word count. First, ruthlessly eliminate peripheral points and details, even if they are interesting or well worded—weak arguments will only dilute the overall impact of your query. Next, consider how many points remain; although up to six strong summary points are fine, more would probably be overkill unless your proposed piece is very long. The *quality* of your points is more important to editors than *quantity*.

Once you've identified the best material, edit it to remove wordy phrasing, awkward constructions, clichés, and stylistic errors. Work on compressing the essence of your ideas into as few words as possible. Give the style a bit of sparkle by varying your sentence structure and length; using vivid, strong verbs; keeping adjectives to a minimum; and putting in a few catchy phrases here and there.

Time spent polishing your summary is time well spent. A strong summary is the heart of an effective sales presentation for your article or book.

ILLUSTRATION 4-1: Lead and Summary: Computers Around the House

Is there a computer in your future? The odds are better than 50/50 that you'll own a "personal" or "home" computer by the end of the decade, say many experts. The home computer industry, which didn't exist before 1975, is one of the fastest-growing businesses in the United States. Last year, Americans spent $1.5 billion on home computers; this year the figure is expected to double.

The tremendous boom in home computers is happening for two reasons. One is price: Unlike most consumer products, computers are actually getting cheaper each year. A computer that would have cost $1 million in 1946 costs less than $1,000 today. The second reason is performance: The computer of 1946 filled several rooms, used enough electricity to power a small apartment building, and required around-the-clock maintenance. Today's computer fits on a desktop, uses no more electricity than a light bulb, and needs little maintenance. A comparable improvement in the automobile would have us driving Rolls Royces that get three million miles to the gallon and sell for $1.50.

A home computer can be put to an enormous variety of uses. It can balance your checkbook, figure out your income taxes, teach you a foreign language, keep track of your appointments, plan menus, maintain inventories, play an astonishing variety of games, control household appliances, type error-free letters, draw pictures and charts, play and compose music, even speak to you in recognizable English.

Best of all, these new computers are easy enough for a child to use. In fact, many parents are now using them to educate their children. No special expertise is required; loading today's "user-friendly" software is as simple as putting a record on your stereo.

Because of its affordable price, great power, and widespread availability, the home computer is fated to become as popular as TV is now. Networks of home computers could form a new medium of communication, sending and receiving "electronic mail"; bringing the library to the living room via telephone access to information data bases; and creating the "electronic cottage" where your computer pays your bills, comparison shops for all household needs, orders repairs, saves energy, and fixes dinner and perhaps a cocktail. Home computers are the vanguard of a technological revolution that is putting the computer—and its power—within the reach of every American.

Chapter 5

Selling Yourself

Once you've sold the editor on the merits of your proposed article, it's important to deliver a strong pitch for *yourself* as a writer and expert. Since a strong presentation of your background is a critical link in the sales chain—would you commit your firm's money to hiring a stranger you know nothing about?—don't neglect your author's biography (usually abbreviated to *bio*). If you've yet to sell your first piece, your bio can help you make that crucial first sale by proving to the editor that you're worth taking a chance on. Have a few sales already? The right bio can make those accomplishments register powerfully on an editor, helping you boost your article rates.

Wondering what qualifications to mention? My writing students, most of whom are unpublished when they start my courses, often worry about their lack of writing credits, not realizing that an effective bio need not be a list of the author's previous publications. *Other* credentials, such as job-related skills or life experience, can be used to construct a powerful, impressive bio.

ANATOMY OF AN AUTHOR

To decide what aspects of your life and experience to highlight in your bio, look for relevant information in these areas:

Your Job. Does your job involve writing? Putting out the company newsletter or writing press releases, technical material, or advertising copy are all examples of a writing background that could be helpful in marketing your articles. Here's how you might describe this experience in your author's bio: "As publicity director for Wondra Cosmetics, I have written hundreds of press releases, many of which were published verbatim in such newspapers as the *Dallas Morning News*, the *New York Post*, and the *Kansas City Star*."

If any of the materials you've written on the job connect at all with your query topic, include photocopies with your query.

Editing experience is another on-the-job skill worth mentioning in your query. If you hold or have held an editorial position, include your title if it's impressive, or describe your responsibilities for positions lower on the corporate ladder. Be specific: "My publishing background includes five years on the editorial staff of Berkley Books, where I assisted in the editing of such best-sellers as . . .," or "For the past three years, I've written, edited, and done layout for our annual report, distributed to 30,000 shareholders."

If current or past jobs tie in to your query topic, explain the connection: "As a former nursery school teacher of 11 years' experience, I have developed many insights into 'Selecting the Right Preschool for Your Child.' " When describing relevant work experience, mention your title and employer (if reasonably impressive) and the length of your tenure in the position (unless very brief). It never hurts to drop names, so if you worked closely with any prominent people or had impressive accounts, work the names into your bio if possible.

Is your position uncommonly powerful or influential? A high-status job as, for example, an upper executive, medical doctor, psychologist, lawyer, college professor, or government official, combined with a powerful article presentation, suggests to an editor that your success in one professional arena might well translate into another—writing. Reinforce this impression by mentioning any professional honors or awards you may have received.

Spectacular *failure* can sometimes be a selling point, as well, particularly for business advice, humor, or personal experience pieces. Here's an example: "I am particularly well qualified to write on 'Going Bust with Style,' since I was voted 'Most Likely to Fail' by my high school class after going bankrupt at the tender age of 17 (debts $290,000; assets $120). Your readers can profit from the expensive education I received during my first attempt at entrepreneurship. . . ."

Your Education.   If you've attended courses on your article topic or have a degree in the field, describe your academic background, mentioning the name of the college or university if particularly prestigious. *Any* degree beyond B.A. or B.S., even if it doesn't touch directly on your article subject, could be a potential qualification worth mentioning in the bio.

One form of education best *omitted* from your bio is a list of writing courses attended. Such references tend to emphasize your lack of writing experience.

Editors should be interested in any teaching or speaking you've done on your topic or closely related subjects, whether as a college or adult education instructor, seminar or workshop leader, or paid lecturer: "My article will draw from my successful Rochelle Adult Center course, 'How to Find a Husband in 10 Days,' which has attracted more than 500 students in the past two semesters." If possible, send a photocopy of your course listing from the school catalog or seminar brochure as further ammunition.

Life Experience.   Even if you aren't planning to write a first-person account, citing direct personal experience you've had with the subject is frequently a good sales tactic. If your article will discuss "Divorce Mediation—Is It For You?," an effective biographical statement (if true) would be: "I am highly familiar with the pros and cons of mediation, having just completed a mediated divorce."

Since editors want writers to be sensitive to the needs of the audience of their magazines, pointing out how you match the reader profile is sound strategy: "Since I returned to work when my first-born was just 3 months old, finding quality childcare has always been an important priority with me. My article will draw from my experiences with housekeepers, au pairs, family day care, and child care centers."

Your Hobbies.   Formal study is not the only route to expertise. A strong interest in the subject can be an excellent qualification in itself. As an enthusiastic amateur, one of my clients was able to sell his book on home computers despite his lack of either computer-related jobs or writing experience of any sort. Instead, his bio described how he built a computer from scratch, collected dozens of computer magazines and books, and attended computer shows all over the country. Publishers found this recital so convincing that three houses participated in an auction for his book.

To use this approach effectively, cite as much evidence of your interest as possible: "Antique dolls have been a passion of mine for more than 20 years. My collection, acquired at a cost of $1,500, now contains more than 200 dolls and was recently valued at $25,000. My doll-collecting library includes 45 books and 300 magazine articles on the subject, as well as many catalogs and dealer addresses."

Your Family. Mentioning family members can be a good strategy in some queries. Your spouse's expertise—or that of another relative—could be cited to augment your own: "Since my husband owns a contracting business, Kitchens Unlimited, I'll be able to provide many professional secrets in 'Slash Your Remodeling Costs.'"

Your family situation could be used to demonstrate your familiarity with the subject: "My wife and I have just adopted two Korean children, so are well versed in 'The Foreign Adoption Maze.'" Just *having* a spouse or child could be a strong qualification for other articles: "As a new bride, I have experienced and overcome 'The Honeymoon Blues,' so I can address the topic with authority" would be a helpful bio item in a submission to *Bride's* magazine.

Your Friends. Like family members, friends can be cited as authorities to be consulted for the article. If friends are also experts, you may wish to omit the relationship and simply list them in the summary among the other sources you plan to interview. On the other hand, if your friends are in a position to supply insider detail, describing them as intimates could be helpful: "Since two of my friends recently decamped from the Children of Love cult, I'll have access to much first-hand material about the group, as well as some surprising revelations."

Friends can be potential examples and case histories, too: "Several of my friends have recently tried videodating, with mixed results, and have offered to contribute anecdotes about their dating adventures."

Your Sins. If your past is a bit shady, you may want to confess in your bio, when appropriate. Among the clients I've represented are a self-admitted cocaine smuggler, call girl, rock groupie, and con man. I've often been asked if you can get into trouble by admitting to criminal activities in print. Though your wisest move is to discuss your specific situation with a good lawyer, those of my clients who've sought legal advice on the subject have been told that a bit of vagueness about exact dates and places is the key to preventing possible hassles with the law.

Is your proposed article more in the nature of a kiss-and-tell piece about your romantic or erotic experiences? Be sure to avoid potential libel by disguising your leading man or lady, especially if your comments are negative. You may also wish to hide behind a pseudonym for racier material. If so, simply mention your pseudonym somewhere in the bio: "I'll be writing this piece under the name of 'Janice Witherington.' "

Your Publicity.   Have you appeared on radio or TV or received write-ups in the local press? If your media coverage is directly relevant to your proposed article, send the editor copies of any printed materials, marking the places where your name appears. For radio and TV appearances, mention the name of the program, adding a brief description if editors are likely to be unfamiliar with the show: "I have appeared several times on 'Fairfield Exchange,' a local cable show viewed by 300,000 Connecticut residents."

Even if your publicity has no strong connection to your proposed article, there's still a good reason to mention it. Many magazines like to promote themselves by arranging for publicity appearances of authors featured in their magazines. By showing that you have some experience with the media, you show the editor that you are a potentially promotable author.

Other Exhibits.   Copies of your *Who's Who* entry or other biographical listings can also be attached to your query. If you are attaching an exhibit, be sure to refer to it in your bio: "For further biographical details, see the attached listing from *Who's Who in American Women*." Including your resume is usually superfluous. Don't send photos of yourself.

THE WRITE STUFF

What's the best way to present any writing credits you may have? First, decide if the credit should be included. Unless you are very young, omit any high school yearbook credits. College publications might be included, especially if you attended a well-known school or university or your paper has won prestigious awards. Any other credits—newspaper articles; newsletters; magazine pieces; and books you wrote, coauthored, or contributed to—should be included. Here's how to describe your credits:

Books. Since editors are most impressed by the credits most similar to your proposed project, mention your books first in a book query, your articles first in an article query. One exception to this rule is when you are submitting an article query on a topic you've previously written a book on; here the book is your strongest qualification, so should be listed first in this particular article query.

When listing your book credits (if any), give the exact title and publisher (unless it's a vanity publication). You may also wish to describe the book briefly: "My first book, *How to Sell Every Magazine Article You Write*, was published in Fall 1986 by Writer's Digest Books." If you sold more than ten thousand hardcovers or fifty thousand paperbacks, sales figures could be added, along with any book clubs, movie options, foreign translations, and first or second serial sales (magazine excerpts).

One Magazine Credit. If the magazine is relatively obscure, give its name and a capsule description: "My work has appeared in *Canadian Fiction Magazine*, a literary publication." For better-known magazines, just mention the name: "I have been published in *Harper's Bazaar*." If your piece was published in the past year, you may also wish to include the date of publication.

If your published article was similar in style, approach, or subject to the one you are now proposing to write, include a photocopy of the article, stating, "I'm including a sample clip to demonstrate my usual style and approach." If your previous piece was fiction or poetry, do not include a copy. For other nonfiction writing, send a copy unless you feel the editor would get a misleading impression of your style from the previously published piece.

If you've recently sold a piece, but the article has not yet appeared in print, use this phrasing: "I've sold my work to *House Beautiful*." If you know the date of publication, you can write: "I have a piece coming up in the October issue of *Arizona Magazine*." Do not include a copy of such yet-to-be-published material unless the editor who bought it from you gives his or her consent; many magazines don't want the competition to know what they have in the works.

What if your only sale was an assigned piece that was ultimately rejected? Try this wording: "I've written for *Outdoor America.*" Naturally, as you acquire more credits, you'll eliminate such entries in favor of your successful publications.

Two to Nine Magazine Credits.   List them all, starting with the magazine most familiar to the publications you plan to submit the current query to. Better-known magazines should be mentioned before more obscure ones. If you've had several articles in some of the publications, you might want to write up your credits like this: "I've written six articles for *Weight Watchers Magazine;* my pieces have also appeared in *Chess Life, Cape Cod Guide,* and *Frequent Flyer.*" Include copies of one or more recent articles, selecting those most similar to your current topic.

Ten or More Magazine Credits.   Once you build up a lengthy list of credits, you can afford to be selective, tailoring your credit list to reflect the interests of the publication you are currently approaching. You'd word your credit list like this: "I've been published in more than a dozen magazines, including *Penthouse, Glamour, Family Circle, Cosmopolitan,* and *Atlantic Monthly.*"

Newspaper Credits.   After any magazine or book credits, cite newspapers your work has appeared in, indicating the geographical area served if it doesn't appear in the paper's name. Copies of newspaper pieces are not as good samples as previous magazine pieces, but can be included in the absence of other clips. If your news or feature story was syndicated, mention both the syndicate and the number of sales (if known): "United Feature Syndicate has bought several of my pieces, typically selling them to 45 member papers."

Other Writing Credits.   If your list of credits looks a bit slim, you may wish to add minor credits such as newsletters you've written for, sales of fillers (very short magazine items like helpful hints), freelance public relations work, technical writing, copywriting, fliers and brochures, and other forms of writing which you've been paid to do.

POLISHING YOUR BIO

Once you've assembled likely material for your bio, edit it to one paragraph—two if your background is very extensive. Start off with writing credits, if any, then list the remaining information in order of importance, the most interesting point *first*. (For a sample author bio, see the illustration on page 54.) Be sure to include as many specifics as possible, checking spelling of names. Devote the same meticulous attention to your bio as you would to your resume—it's as important to make exactly the right impression when you're seeking a sale as when you're applying for a job.

ILLUSTRATION 5-1: Sample Bio

ELIZABETH TENER

Elizabeth Tener is a freelance journalist who writes frequently about adolescence, psychology, careers, and travel. She is the career columnist for *Self* magazine, and her pieces have appeared in such top national publications as *Bride's, Woman's Day, Reader's Digest, McCall's, Family Circle, Young Miss,* and *Cosmopolitan.* She is the author of *Getting Personal: Finding that Special Someone Through the Classifieds* (Bantam Books, 1985), plus two books for the Research Institute of America: *How to Help Your Children Choose the Right Career* (1985) and *The 1986 Guide to Personal and Business Travel.*

For eight years she was senior editor of *Co-ed,* a magazine for young people published by Scholastic Inc. Her features about teenaged sexuality and pregnancy, drug abuse, alcoholism, and other important social issues won her the Best of Series award from the Educational Press Association of America in 1978, 1981, and 1982.

Ms. Tener received a B.A. degree from Smith College and an M.A.T. from Brown University. She has attended the Bread Loaf Writer's Conference and is a member of the American Society of Journalists and Authors.

Your bio can be written either in the third person, as in this example, or the first person.

Chapter 6

Research and Interview Shortcuts

What makes a query sell? Success comes from creating a winning combination of five crucial elements: appropriate market selection, a fresh idea, a skillful presentation, competent writing, and good research. Each of these components contributes to the sale: Submitting to the most likely markets puts your work in the hands of potential buyers. A good idea, presented effectively and written smoothly, stimulates editorial interest. And a solid foundation of facts in your query helps close the deal, by proving that *you* are the right man or woman for the job.

The reason editors place such a high value on research is that they understand the fundamental appeal of nonfiction: *readers want to learn, as well as be entertained.* The better your facts are, the more satisfying your piece will be—and the more saleable. While some queries can be written entirely from your existing knowledge, most can be enhanced with a bit of digging and interviewing. For your personal experience query, for example, you might want to verify certain details—there's nothing that puts an editor off like detecting an error in your query; supply statistics to demonstrate how common or rare the situation is; or provide background information to increase the editor's understanding of your subject.

Not only can your research and interview material help sell

your story idea, but it can hide a multitude of writing sins. For the new writer who lacks an impressive array of publishing credits, it supplements your bio by showing that you do have the necessary journalistic skills to deliver a good piece. Excellence of information and provocative quotes can also mask weakness of style: I've known many a skillful researcher who has succeeded in the nonfiction field despite mediocre writing skills. Or if your idea is a bit offbeat, your research becomes doubly vital in persuading the editor to sign you up: your facts must overwhelm the editor's initial resistance both to the idea and to you as a new writer.

While the word "research" might convey images of trudging through library stacks, potential sources of information are all around you once you know where—and how—to look.

FACTS AT YOUR FINGERTIPS

Often you can get enough facts to fill a query with a phone call or two. Here are some telephone research ideas:

Call Your Library. Many libraries now offer free telephone reference service. Librarians prefer that you ask just one or two very concise questions: "What's the average age for first marriages in the U.S.?" or "How many homers did Babe Ruth hit in his career?"

Facts aren't all your librarian can give you. You can also verify famous quotations, determine the names of the standard reference books on your subject, obtain a list of organizations devoted to your topic, learn phone numbers of well known people, and find out which library in your area has the best collection on your topic.

Answers That Compute. If you have a home computer and a modem (a telephone hook-up for computers), you can subscribe to an informational data base. To use it, you'd call a special number, enter your access code on your terminal, and select from a menu of data bases that include indices and abstracts of popular magazines, current news events, medical and scientific journals, U.S. and foreign patents, legal literature, and a variety of other specialized sources of information. For more information on data base research, read *Answers Online: Your Guide to Informational Data Bases*, by Barbara Newlin.

For data base bargains, look into services that operate only during off-peak hours (evenings and weekends) for reduced rates. Two such services are: BRS/After Dark (1200 Route 7, Latham, NY 12110) and Knowledge Index (3460 Hillview Ave., Palo Alto, CA 94304). Both services charge a sign-up fee (sometimes with a certain number of hours of free connection time), plus a per-minute rate for connection time. There are no monthly minimums—you only pay for what you use.

If you are not yet "on line," many libraries now provide computerized research for modest fees. You pay only for computer time; there's no charge for the services of the research librarian who helps you define the parameters of your search.

Dial An Expert.   Need some information on traveling with pets, protecting yourself from asbestos in the home, or current salaries in the telecommunications field for your query? Your local yellow pages may be your best research tool. For the price of a local call, you can get a quick interview with professionals who welcome the publicity your article might bring.

Whom should you call? Try local businesses, professionals in the field, associations and clubs, chambers of commerce, tourist bureaus, historic societies, hospitals, and state and federal government agencies.

If you're having trouble finding experts, also check *The Encyclopedia of Associations*, available at your library, for the names of potentially helpful organizations. Not only will many of these groups provide you with facts over the phone, but some will also mail you brochures, booklets, bibliographies, reprints of previous articles on the topic, and even complete books—absolutely free.

THE ARTFUL INTERVIEW

Your interview tactics will depend on whether your goal is to obtain facts or quotes for your query and how much material you actually need. For any piece that will draw heavily from one source, such as a profile article or "as told to" story, interviewing your subject in person is preferable. Most of your interviews, however, will be done over the telephone.

Here's how to get the most out of your interview subjects:

Work From A Script.   Before calling or visiting your informant, prepare a list of questions. If you are most interested in facts and background information, design your questions to elicit exact dates, prices, statistics, names, and other facts. Make the questions short and easy to understand: "How many divorce mediators are now practicing in the United States?" or "What sort of activities do Outward Bound trips include?"

If interesting quotes or anecdotes are your goal, create more thoughtful questions—ones that cannot be answered with a simple yes or no. For articles with a strong slant, you may want to use leading questions to ensure that your source agrees with the point of view presented in the query: "Doctor, speculating about the future of romance, would you say that scientists may locate a 'love gene' that dictates romantic preferences?"

For detailed questioning strategies and additional interview tips, read *The Craft of Interviewing*, by John Brady.

Don't Neglect the Basics.   Unless your subject is very well known, start interviews by verifying the spelling of the subject's name, his or her exact title or preferred description, and the person's professional affiliations. Ask if you can contact your source in the future for additional material. When the questioning is complete, ask if your interviewee has any written materials available on the subject—I was once given an unpublished research paper about a startling medical breakthrough. Also ask for names of other experts you should contact, plus suggestions on a reading list.

Take Notes.   Jot down key points, colorful phrases or descriptions, likely quotes, and any ideas of your own that the interviewee's words may trigger. For in-person interviews, you may wish to tape, but take notes anyway as a backup in case of tape failure and to guide you to the correct portions of the tape. Before taping phone interviews, check with the phone company for applicable regulations in your state.

Double-Check Facts.   Sadly, some experts would rather guess than admit they don't know. Or your subject may simply be mistaken. It's a sensible precaution to verify your interview material with another expert or published material before putting it in your query. This is especially important if your interviewee's statements appear libelous or controversial.

Select and Edit Quotes.   Looking over your notes, select quotes that make points strongly, use vivid imagery, arouse emotion, or use colorful phrasing. For near-miss quotes, feel free to do minor editing to improve grammar or make the words flow smoothly. Be sure you preserve your interviewee's meaning, however. If you perform major surgery on a quote, consult your interviewee before including the recast version.

RESEARCH STRATEGIES

Valuable as research is, you can have too much of a good thing. Wading through every tome ever published on your topic in search of choice morsels to offer editors is overkill; instead, your objective should be to locate just enough information to give your query substance, postponing an in-depth investigation until the piece is actually sold. By keeping query research down, you'll be able to write your queries more quickly, multiplying your sales prospects.

The best way to keep research to a profitable minimum is to organize a research plan before you start looking for material. Start by summarizing your primary topic into a key word or two: "weddings, double," "stuntmen," "Arctic exploration." For complex topics, a brief outline is helpful in identifying key concepts. If your topic were "Money-Saving Strategies," you might decide to cover budget meals, discount travel, clothing bargains, and health maintenance organizations.

Next, decide what sort of facts would be most useful for your query. If you were writing about "Where the Boys Are," you'd probably want to include figures on the male/female ratios in the cities you'd be discussing; a query on "The Psychology of Money" might be enlivened with a few anecdotes about famous spenders and misers.

FINDING THE MOTHER LODE

Here's a systematic approach to library research:

Start With Magazines.   *Magazine Index* is available on microfilm readers at most libraries. Similar to *Reader's Guide to Periodical Literature*, this guide covers about 400 popular magazines, like *Cosmopoli-*

tan and *Psychology Today.* It's organized by subject; within each heading you'll find the most recently published piece listed first—helpful if your goal is to get the latest information only.

Since *Magazine Index* covers only the past several years, if you need to consult older articles, use the volume of *Reader's Guide to Periodical Literature* corresponding to the dates that interest you. For specialized publications, check such indices as *Business Periodicals Index, Psychological Abstracts, Index Medicus,* and other subject directories.

To get best results, be imaginative in your key words. In researching an article on danger, I found material under "risk," "mountaineering," "sports," "adrenaline," "exploration," "courage," and "safety." Try to find at least two good articles on the topic.

Magazine Index can also be a good tool for submission planning (discussed in more detail in chapter 9). You'll see at a glance which magazines in your field of interest have covered the topic recently and which have not, making it easy to see which are the best submission bets. (As a general rule, it's best to try your query on publications that haven't covered the topic in the previous two years, unless your slant differs drastically from previous pieces.)

Check Vertical Files. Many libraries maintain files of booklets and clippings on selected topics. All of your query research could be waiting in one of these folders. To find them, either ask the librarian for assistance or look for them on the library shelves where books on the topic are placed. They are usually at the end of a row.

Try Newspapers. Newspaper articles are excellent research tools, since they tend to be terse and fact-filled and to quote local experts, giving you potential leads on sources you could contact. To find them, check *Newspaper Index,* which covers 1979 to the present. You'll find listings from *The New York Times* and *Wall Street Journal* and a few others.

Skim a Book or Two. Although booklets and magazine or newspaper pieces are preferable to books for query research because they are shorter and may be more up-to-date, a good book on the topic may draw together information from diverse sources that would be hard to find quickly on your own.

To locate helpful books quickly, simply check the library's card catalog to identify which Library of Congress or Dewey decimal numbers are assigned to your subject, and do your selecting directly from the bookshelves. The best way to evaluate which books will be most useful is to scan the flap copy and table of contents, then flip to the index to see how many pages are devoted to the topics that interest you. Read a page at random to see whether the style and approach appeal to you. The footnotes, bibliography, and appendices may be valuable sources of new research leads—I've often found good articles on the topic this way and learned of new organizations to contact.

In addition to books exclusively about your subject, you may also want to glance at almanacs, yearbooks, books of lists, and other collected works. Some reference books I use frequently are *Guinness Book of World Records*, *The American Almanac of Jobs and Salaries*, and *The World Almanac*.

KNOWING WHEN TO QUIT

When should you stop researching and start writing? Many inexperienced writers over-research their queries and articles because they are unsure when to stop. While it's impossible to avoid some wasted effort in research—you can't really tell how valuable a source will be until you've examined it—I've established some rough guidelines for research efficiency:

• Always try to get the information by telephone first. Quickie phone interviews are the most efficient research method for queries.

• One source may be enough if it's absolutely reliable; two should be sufficient for most queries. Sources can either be experts or published materials, or a combination of both.

• Don't chase down every lead; stop when you have enough for your query. A certain percentage of the potential research will be unavailable at your library; it's rarely worth going to other libraries or making repeat trips for these missing links. If you really want a certain publication, however, your library can frequently borrow it through an interlibrary loan.

• Whenever possible, combine research for several projects into one library trip. Also, by planning several articles on a topic, you can get more mileage out of your experts and reading.

- Photocopy as much of your research material as possible while you are at the library, instead of taking notes. Don't read the whole piece on the spot, just check the first couple of paragraphs for relevance, then photocopy. Take lots of change.

- Read your research materials in your spare time—during the commute to work, waiting in line at the bank, while you're holding for a phone caller. Read quickly, marking any interesting passages for easy reference as you write.

- Make a habit of clipping any newspaper or magazine articles that intrigue you as a starting point for future projects.

- If cost permits, consider buying reference books you find you use frequently.

- Keep working to upgrade your research and interviewing techniques. I'm constantly discovering new sources of information at the library and devising ways to shorten phone interviews to the minimum. The faster you work—without sacrificing quality—the more quickly you can get your queries to editors and the sooner you'll start ringing up some sales.

Chapter 7

Letter Perfect

Your query is almost ready to submit now. The final step is to add an air of professionalism with judicious editing, followed by meticulous typing and formatting. Though even the most stylish presentation won't sell a bad idea, it's especially important for a new writer to make a positive first impression. Studies show that a durable opinion is formed within the first fifteen *seconds* of acquaintance—making it vital that you introduce yourself to the magazine, via your query, in just the right way.

Once you've written the three key sections of your query—the lead, summary, and bio—use this five-step editing approach to produce a final draft:

Keep It Concise.   Editors prefer short, punchy queries. If yours is more than two double-spaced pages in length, cutting is frequently indicated. However, if your query is crammed with interesting, important information, a slightly longer query is often acceptable; I've sold some articles with queries of two and a half or even three pages.

Even if length doesn't appear to be a problem, trimming the fat will often improve your query substantially; you may be telling the editor too much. Your lead should be confined to one to two paragraphs, the summary to three to six major points, and the bio to one paragraph—two if your background is uncommonly impressive.

Eliminate minor ideas and less impressive sales points. Weak material dilutes the overall impact of your query and may cause the editor's attention to wander. It's better to say too little than too much; interested editors will often ask for more material if necessary.

Fill the Gaps.   After removing any weak links in the chain of ideas, make sure you haven't left out anything important. If, for example, your piece is titled "The Seven Reasons Children Fail in School," each of the reasons should be mentioned briefly. Obvious as this advice may sound, I've seen students in my writing course omit equally vital information from their queries.

Occasionally, I've encountered writers who deliberately withhold key information as a sales device, reasoning that the editor might want to buy the query to learn the full story. A few writers are stingy with facts out of fear of having their ideas stolen by editors. This misguided approach will harm your odds of selling; a query shouldn't tell all—that's the job of an article—but it should certainly clue the editor in as to what your story is all about by highlighting your major points.

Organize and Clarify.   Now that you've got content right, consider whether the material is arranged logically and written clearly. Your title should either precede the query text or be included somewhere in the first paragraph. It's important also to state your exact topic early in the query—you don't want to confuse the editor or have her misunderstand your ideas. If you introduce your topic with an anecdote or description, make sure a clear statement of purpose follows: "The article will demystify home mortgages, with detailed explanations of widely available plans and easy-to-use formulas for comparing different terms and rates quickly."

For your summary, start strong with a powerful point, and arrange all subsequent points in order of interest. To avoid closing with your least interesting point, reserve a "clincher" for last. If A is the best point and E the least important, the correct arrangement is: A, C, D, E, B. Use the same organization for your bio.

To increase clarity and create an attractive layout, you may wish to use "bullet formation" for longer summaries. Here's an example from a query I wrote on "Quitting With Style":

The article will cover:
● Strategies to salvage your existing job—making a mini-

job hunt within the company, using your threat to resign as a negotiating point, presenting your grievances coolly and effectively.

● Reading the handwriting on the wall—signs that tell you to quit.

● Planning your reentry—evaluating your transferable skills, investigating new fields, discreet ways to look for a job while you still have one.

● Parting with panache—writing your resignation letter, handling the exit interview, and other tips on leaving a positive impression on your boss, plus strategies to garner references and referrals from coworkers.

● Avoiding the no-paycheck crunch—financial strategies.

● The postparting period—how to beat the no-job blues while you search for the best spot for your talents.

Sharpen Your Style.   The style tips for better leads given in chapter 3 will also improve your overall style in the query, and can be equally effective as an editorial checklist for completed articles.

Here are two areas of the query letter whose style warrants special attention.

Opening Flourishes: If you've selected the traditional letter query as your format, you'll usually need an opening line before you launch into your lead. Here's a first paragraph I frequently use:

> I'd like to propose an article for *Family Circle*, "The 10 Best Jobs to Get Rich." Here's how I'd handle it:

Once I've mentioned the name of the publication I'm submitting to and my title, I move directly to my lead, summary, and bio. If you have a special sales point you want to emphasize, you can work it into this introductory paragraph:

> I enjoyed *Savvy's* recent piece on making a winning first impression. My proposed article addresses this subject from a different viewpoint; "In Her Image" focuses on women who've successfully overcome serious image problems in the office. Here's how I'll approach it:

Exit Lines: Drawing your letter query to a graceful close is equally important. As every good salesperson knows, the most effective way to end a sales presentation is by *asking for the sale.* Here are three closing lines that I use frequently.

- *I'll look forward to your reaction.*   I like this one because I think it conveys an attitude of cheerful expectation and confidence.

- *Since this project is very timely, I'll hope for your speedy response.*   This one works best if your idea is genuinely urgent.

- *What do you think?*   This strikes me as a snappy way to close a longer query. It gets right to the point.

Your close could be tailored to the topic of your query. If, for example, you're writing about a topic with a very broad appeal, you might want to finish with something like, "Since one out of six couples is currently infertile, my infertility handbook should attract a wide readership." For lighter topics, try a note of humor at the end, as Amy Sunshine Genova does in the illustration on page 34, or bring up timing considerations: "My procrastination piece might be a good bet for your August issue, when readers are confronting the summer doldrums."

As a final quality check, read your query aloud. You'll notice which sentences flow smoothly, which are awkwardly phrased. Rework and polish until you are completely satisfied that you've expressed yourself well.

Perfect With Proofreading.   Check, double-check, and triple-check. Sloppy spelling, errors of fact, and haphazard punctuation or grammar signal a lack of professionalism, making editors hesitant to trust you with assignments. Though a few trivial errors probably won't affect your odds of a sale, why create a negative impression?

A common error to watch for in your style is the excessive use of quotation marks or exclamation points. There's no need to use quotes around slang expressions, as some writers do; reserve quotes for direct quotations and unfamiliar expressions you are about to define. Relying on exclamation points suggests that you are trying to make punctuation do the work of your writing; instead, rephrase the sentence to convey the excitement you feel.

For best proofreading results, let the query age overnight before making a final check. You'll be surprised how many more errors you notice when you freshen your perspective with a good night's rest.

If you are weak in spelling, grammar, or punctuation, you can recruit a proofreader from among your friends or family members.

Or give yourself a cram course in usage by conscientious study of such books as *The Handbook of Current English*, by Jim W. Corder and John J. Ruszkiewicz, which I've found invaluable in my work, or one of the two favorite style books of the magazine world, *The Chicago Manual of Style* and *The New York Times Manual of Style and Usage.*

THE LOOK OF SUCCESS

Your query is now ready for final typing in a format suitable for submission. Be sure to use a fresh cloth ribbon or film cartridge for crisp, sharp lettering. Check if your typewriter keys need cleaning—editors dislike smudgy copy. Computer-printed submissions are now quite acceptable, but be sure the printer you select prints with the quality of a typewriter. Each character should be dark and clear, and the type style should show letters such as y and g with their tails below the line.

Your typing paper should be a medium-weight bond. Editors dislike erasable paper, which smudges easily and leaves ink on the reader's fingers. White or cream-colored papers are equally appropriate for queries or manuscripts. Pica and elite are both acceptable type sizes. Always use black ribbons; any other color will strike the editor as amateurish, as will italic type.

CHOOSING YOUR FORMAT

You have a choice of two widely used formats for your query. The traditional approach is to structure your query as a conventional business letter, typed entirely in single spacing and laid out as in the illustration on page 70. A newer approach is to use *two* documents: a covering letter, in the format of a business letter (see the illustration on page 72) and a separate query, typed in manuscript format (see the illustration on page 73). The two-document query has a single-spaced cover letter and a double-spaced query manuscript.

Both formats have their pros and cons, but they are equally accepted by editors. The letter query is friendly and personal, but inconvenient for multiple submissions since the entire text must be retyped for each submission if you're not using word processing. It is flexible, though, because you can alter the text of the query to reflect editorial preferences at each publication you submit to.

The two-document query sacrifices some of the personal touch, since the covering letter is all that you'll change for each submission, inserting new sales points, references to recent articles in that publication, and other points of interest to that particular publication. The actual query can be photocopied for easy multiple submissions; keep the original at home so you can have fresh copies run off whenever necessary.

The letter query is best for unique submissions, very short queries, and occasions when a personal approach is desired, such as submissions to editors you know well. Otherwise, the advantages of using the two-document query outweigh its slightly impersonal quality.

Multiple Idea Queries.   If you're submitting two or more ideas to the same editor in a single submission, separate queries are the best choice. Different editors within the magazine may specialize in such topics as health, fashion, or interviews; separate queries make it simple for the editor who receives your submission to refer ideas that fall outside her province to others within the company.

Each query should have your name, address, and phone number on the first page. That way, if different editors end up considering your ideas, each one has all the information needed to contact you should he or she be interested in commissioning the piece. However, a single covering letter can be attached to the queries. Make sure it briefly identifies each one by title, with a line or two of description.

Letters to the Editor.   When you're presenting a query/cover letter combination, your first priority is identifying which points to feature in your cover letter and which to reserve for the attached query. It's best to keep your cover letter quite brief—your goal is to pique the editor's interest in the query, *not* to give information that will be repeated in the query.

Start by mentioning your title, with a brief explanation if your topic and slant can't be readily divined from the title alone: "Enclosed is my query, 'High Finance,' about cocaine use among Wall Street fast-trackers."

Next, mention any points of special interest to that particular publication: "I've noticed over the past year that *Self* has been emphasizing pregnancy articles, so my piece on 'Postpartum Sex' should interest many of your readers." Comments like this show the editor you are highly familiar with his publication, suggesting that you can be expected to turn in a piece that will be targeted on the magazine's readership.

If you can truthfully say that you are a regular reader of the magazine, this should also be mentioned in the cover letter. When I approached *Cosmopolitan* for the first time, I wrote, "I've been reading and enjoying *Cosmo* since I was a teenager." The result? An assignment that proved to be the beginning of a long and profitable relationship with the magazine.

If you have been referred socially by a regular contributor or an editor at the magazine or book publishing company, you may also wish to explain the connection: "Your sales manager, Frederick K. Smythe, is my next-door neighbor. He suggested that I contact you about this book project."

One or two special sales points can also be included in the cover letter, but make sure you don't repeat the same information in your query. If your background or expertise is quite impressive, you might decide to highlight your bio by moving it to the cover letter, rather than positioning it at the end of your query.

Like a letter query, a cover letter should end with a request for the editor's reaction.

With a bit of work and the right strategies, you're likely to find that one of your queries produces the best reaction of all—an article sale.

ILLUSTRATION 7-1: Letter Query

(date)

Ms. Rona Cherry
Executive Editor
Glamour
350 Madison Ave.
New York, NY 10017

Dear Ms. Cherry:

"SIDS: The Sudden Killer of Infants Younger than a Year" is the title of an article I'd like to write. It will be a personal account, containing much factual information, of a family who suffered the tragic loss of their second child due to SIDS (sudden infant death syndrome). SIDS is the leading cause of infant mortality in babies over one month of age, claiming about 7,000 victims a year in the United States. One out of 500 babies born this year will die of it.

Michael's delivery, just three days before Christmas, was rapid, easy, and uneventful. At birth he was given a perfect score on the Apgar test (a rating system of the health of a newborn) and was soon discharged from the hospital, an apparently normal child. For the first month of his life, he enjoyed perfect health. On the morning of his death, he woke hungry, fed at his mother's breast, and fell back to sleep. Two hours later, he was dead. There was no warning, no struggle, no sign of illness. Attempts at cardiopulmonary resuscitation by his father, an M.D., failed, and he was pronounced dead on arrival at the hospital. An autopsy revealed that he was a victim of that mysterious killer of babies, SIDS.

The days that followed were agony for his parents: selecting a small casket, arranging a funeral, coping with the worries and fears of their surviving two-year-old, their own guilt at being unable to save their baby, the constant reminders of the brief life that had been extinguished.

Throughout these early days of grief they were not alone. The SIDS Foundation, a national foundation started by the parents of a SIDS victim, provides solace through a caseworker/nurse and counseling sessions. This foundation has chapters in major cities across the United States.

The article will chronicle this family's struggle to rebuild their lives, culminating with the decision to have another baby. (The available evidence suggests that the risk of recurrence is only fractionally higher in a subsequent sibling of a victim than in the general population.)

These are the facts about SIDS:
The victim of SIDS is most likely to be a healthy, well nourished baby, a

second- or thirdborn child, of lower than average birth weight. More infants die in the winter than the summer; more victims are born to mothers who smoke than to nonsmokers, and about half of the victims have previously experienced periods of sleep apnea (long pauses between breaths while sleeping). Most victims die silently during sleep. About half of the victims have had a slight cold prior to death. The SIDS victim is most likely to be between one and four months of age; few victims are over six months of age.

SIDS has been known to strike one baby, leaving a twin brother or sister in the same bed untouched. It is not contagious and poses no risk to others in the household. The disease has been known since Biblical times, when it was called "overlaying" because it was thought that the sleeping mother had rolled on the child, causing suffocation. Actually, neither choking nor suffocation is a cause of SIDS, as had been theorized in the past. SIDS parents have also been suspected of child abuse and even jailed, due to lack of understanding of this mysterious disorder. It is important that accurate information about SIDS become known to avoid such compounding of the tragedy of a SIDS death.

Infants who have shown signs of sleep apnea can be equipped with special monitors which signal abnormalities of breathing or heartbeat, alerting parents to the need for resuscitation. Many high-risk babies have been saved as a result of these monitors. With more research, it is to be hoped that better methods of detection will prevent these tragic infant deaths.

[My bio appeared here.] The article will run about 2,000 to 2,500 words.

Sincerely yours,

Lisa Collier Cool

Letter queries can be typed on letterhead stationery, as this one was, or on plain bond paper. This article sold to *Glamour* for $1,200.

ILLUSTRATION 7-2: Cover Letter

MARY TWELL JOURDIN
970 Rockwell Blvd.
Santana, FL 33129
(305) 555-5671 (office)
(305) 555-4370 (home)

June 19, 1987

Ms. Eileen Maguire
Managing Editor
Parents Magazine
685 Third Ave.
New York, NY 10017

Dear Ms. Maguire:

Enclosed is a query, "Twin Pregnancy." Since one out of 90 pregnancies now results in multiple birth—and the numbers are rising with increased use of fertility drugs and greater numbers of pregnancies during the "twin-prone" years of age 35 and up—many of your readers should be interested in the topic.

Included in the query are an author's bio and full details on the proposed article. I'll just add that I am a mother of twins myself, and former president of the Santana Mothers of Twins and Triplets Club. I'll look forward to your reaction with interest.

Sincerely yours,

Mary Twell Jourdin

The author's name and address are centered to resemble letterhead stationery. For a short letter like this, paragraphs can be either square, as shown here, or indented.

ILLUSTRATION 7-3: Separate Query

Lynette Palmers
78 Mysterious Dr.
Freedom, ME 04901
(207) 555-9999

GETTING MARRIED IN THE 1980s

by

Lynette Palmers

This article would be a three-parter with lots of little boxes containing bulleted tips, helpful hints, bits of wedding lore, checklists. I would have loved to have had this article handy when I got married in 1979 and am sure your readers would find it both helpful and entertaining.

Here's the basic plan of organization:

● Part I, "Getting Engaged"—How to propose to a man . . . the most romantic proposals of all time . . . good buys on engagement rings and tips on designing your own ring . . . enjoying your in-laws—how to make a winning impression.

● Part II, "Planning Your Wedding"—schedule and "who pays for what" . . . selecting a gown . . . double weddings and other unusual situations . . . the most offbeat weddings ever . . . etiquette guide . . . shower ideas.

● Part III, "I do, I do!"—writing your own vows and ceremony . . . gift ideas for the groom and attendants . . . good honeymoon bargains and travel ideas

. . . how to write a thank-you note . . . the name dilemma.

If desired, additional boxes could cover such topics as wedding superstitions or the origins of various traditions like the bridal bouquet (originally garlic and strong-smelling herbs to scare off evil spirits).

I see it as a major piece, 4,500 words in length. I've written several wedding articles in the past—*Modern Bride* bought two, and some local papers ran a New York wedding guide article I wrote a while ago.

If the query is running long, omit the extra spaces between bulleted items.

Chapter 8

Querying Agents and Book Publishers

Do you have a good idea for a nonfiction book? Whether your book is still in the planning stage, consists of a few chapters and an outline, or is fully completed, a query is the best way to approach publishers and literary agents. It's increasingly common for nonfiction authors—even those without previous publishing credits—to sell unwritten books by query or proposal. If you've already written some or all of the book, a query allows you to contact many potential buyers quickly and at minimal cost.

One key difference between book queries and article queries is that the former have greater flexibility about length. Since a book is much longer and more complex than an article, book editors and literary agents are willing to consider longer queries—one to five pages is the usual range. Or you can present the material in a book proposal, which is a more detailed query, running five to fifty pages.

Many authors use both a query and a proposal—the shorter query is sent initially, with the proposal following after the editor or agent has expressed interest. This two-pronged attack gets faster answers—it takes less time to read a query than a proposal, saves on postage, and eliminates the need to write a proposal if the subject doesn't provoke editorial interest.

Your book query can be structured as either a letter addressed to an editor or agent (see the illustration on page 80) or as a covering letter attached to a separate query (see the illustration on page 82). Either format is acceptable to agents and publishers.

THE THREE KEYS TO SUCCESS

Like a magazine query, your book query will revolve around three key components: the lead, summary, and author's bio. Your opening can be either a snappy magazine-type lead, such as an anecdote or series of bulleted items, or a more straightforward statement of purpose, briefly describing the topic of the book.

Once you have identified your subject, you can summarize the book in one of three ways. The simplest is to provide a table of contents, giving the title and a one- or two-sentence description of each chapter. If you haven't settled on the final contents yet, a list of highlights can also be effective. A third approach is to describe the book more informally, in paragraphs developing the key ideas. Using bullets for your chapter-by-chapter summary or highlights list will add emphasis.

For your author's bio, mention any previous book credits, whether fiction or nonfiction, first; followed by other publishing credits (magazines, newspapers, newsletters, movie scripts). If you lack such credits, concentrate on demonstrating your expertise through references to relevant professional or personal experience with the subject.

NUTS AND BOLTS

In either your cover letter or the text of your letter query, include these important points:

Word Count.   Specify the number of words in your book, rounded off to the nearest 5,000. Four double-spaced manuscript pages of 25 lines apiece in pica type usually contain 1,000 words, so a quick way to calculate is to divide the number of pages by four and add three zeros to the result: 500 pages equals 125,000 words.

If the book is not yet written, estimate the number of words as a range: 50,000 to 60,000 would be a short book; 75,000 to 80,000 would be average; 100,000 or more would be long. While publishers don't often buy books that are less than 50,000 words, there's no upward limit to length. The length should be determined by the importance and complexity of your material. Two hundred thousand words would be far too much for a book on lawn cultivation, but not unreasonable for a biography of the Kennedy clan.

Delivery Date. If you haven't written the book yet, indicate the number of months required to complete the book. Most authors take six to eight months to write an average-length or shorter book. Unless your book is very long or requires extensive research, it's best to promise delivery in twelve or fewer months.

Illustrations. Indicate the number of illustrations (if any) you will deliver, and the type of material: "I'll include twenty to thirty stock-performance charts," or "The book will contain seventy-five black and white photos."

If you think the book would be enhanced by illustration but you lack the skill or time to do it yourself, there are two ways to handle this: You can team up with an artist or photographer; briefly describe his or her professional background in your query. If you haven't selected an illustrator, your query could simply contain a line or two about the kind of illustration you'd prefer. Many publishers have lists of freelance illustrators and can match you up with a suitable one once your book is under contract.

Photos and illustrations can also be bought from such services as AP Wide World Photos and the Bettman Archives. *Literary Market Place* has lists of stock photo agencies, photographers, and art services. There's no need to acquire illustrations until your book is under contract, but you may want to check with such services to determine if appropriate material is available.

Foreword. If some distinguished individual has offered to write your introduction, this is a good selling point to include in your query. Give the person's name and a brief biographical sketch.

Format. For heavily illustrated books or works where an unusual graphic treatment is envisioned, you may wish to include ideas about format in your query: "Each subject will be given a four-page photo spread, with brief interview text as captions."

If you have a background in production (say at an advertising agency), you may also want to offer to provide cover art and camera-ready layouts of each page in the book. The publisher will give you a production budget for such services. A few writers also specify paper stock (for a photo book, for example) or the actual dimensions of the book (only if the size you have in mind is quite unusual). But most authors don't involve themselves in production and merely supply typewritten text.

Exhibits. Your query can be enhanced by such extras as copies of recent magazine or newspaper coverage of the subject, any published articles you've done on this subject or closely related ones, text of the book's introduction or first chapter, or articles or excerpts from books mentioning you.

Other suitable attachments include course listings of seminars or workshops you teach, relevant testimonials (such as letters from satisfied customers who've tried the methods you outline in the book query), affidavits and official documents confirming controversial points, and sample photos or illustrations.

OVER THE PUBLISHING TRANSOM

Since each book is a unique product, the secret of a successful query is to *prove* that there's a large enough market for your book to justify adding the book to a publisher's list. Most large hardcover publishers don't consider it economically feasible to publish a work that will sell fewer than ten thousand copies. For trade paperbacks—the more expensive, larger-sized paperback books—minimum sales for publication are about fifteen thousand, while mass market paperback publishers figure on a minimum of fifty thousand sales.

To convince a publisher or agent that the market is there, a bit of research is helpful. If your topic were *Child Care in the '80s,* your query might point out that your target audience is the parents of America's sixty-four million children. Since the overwhelming majority of your projected audience will *not* buy your book—it's rare for any book to sell more than one million copies—the group you identify must be very large to excite the publisher's interest.

Think of your audience in the broadest possible terms. Is it likely that teachers might be interested? What about social workers? Child care attendants? Look also for groups or organizations serving your target audience, and cite membership figures. You may also wish to mention the subscription level of specialized magazines serving this audience; publishers might consider these good targets for promotional efforts or advertisements for the book.

Another indication of the potential demand for your proposed book is the previous success of other books within the genre, if any. For example, the great success of such true crime books as *Blood and Money* and *Fatal Vision* might be cited as a sales point for *your* true crime subject. Exact sales figures for such works can sometimes be gleaned from best-seller lists in *Publishers Weekly*.

If you compare your book to others in the same field of interest, make sure that you demonstrate how your work differs from previous material on the topic. While a few publishers will buy a "me-too" book, most are not interested in putting out carbon copies of classics in the field. You may wish to point out deficiencies in existing works or show how your book complements the existing literature on the subject.

Subsidiary rights potential is another selling point. Might your book be excerpted in major magazines or through newspaper syndicates? Is there any evidence that readers in major European countries or Japan might be interested? What about movie prospects— have similar books found their way to either the big or small screen recently? The likelihood of library sales or book club deals will also get publishers' money antennae waving.

Don't neglect the promotional prospects. Have you ever appeared on either radio or TV or been written up in magazines or newspapers? Cite this media attention as evidence of your promotability as an author. Also, indicate any potential tie-ins to future events—for example, your book on *Romance in America* would get greater attention if published on Valentine's Day.

The existence of specialized markets for your book can also be cited in the query. If, for example, your book is on *Bicycle Repair*, your query could include figures on the number of bike shops in America—these stores might be willing to carry your book. Some publishers are more interested in special sales than others, but it never hurts to mention nontraditional markets.

After you've researched and compiled your list of sales points, select the strongest to include in your query. Remember, quality, not quantity, is the key to a convincing pitch. Then give the rest of the query the same careful editing—the next chapter will alert you to some common pitfalls to avoid.

ILLUSTRATION 8-1: Letter Query for a Book

RORY C. FOSTER, D.V.M.
[address and phone number]

Lisa Collier
Collier Associates
[address]

Dear Ms. Collier:

I've recently completed a manuscript entitled *Wild Patients I Have Known*, which describes my wildlife veterinary experiences from 1977 to 1982. It covers some of my frustrations and triumphs working with injured wild animals. The foreword is written by Dr. Michael Fox, a well known veterinarian and author.

The wildlife rehabilitation field is relatively new in the United States. Most states now have several organizations dealing with injured wildlings, each with several hundreds or even thousands of members. A bird rehab project in Florida, the Suncoast Seabird Sanctuary, currently has more than seven thousand members. California has more than fifty groups dedicated to assisting injured wild creatures! The majority of these American organizations are less than three years old. Since my book would be the first of its kind, I believe that it could become to this movement what Rachael Carson's *Silent Spring* was to the environmental movement of the sixties.

I have enclosed several recent newspaper articles about our project in Wisconsin, along with a recent article from *People* magazine about wildlife rehabilitation in your own state. These articles and hundreds more like them illustrate the powerful public interest in the treatment of injured wild animals.

As these articles demonstrate, there's a wide audience for my book: veterinarians, rehabilitators, and anyone interested in wildlife, doctors, or the intriguing controversy found within the pages of the book. I am firmly committed to the book and its success: I am prepared to take up to one year completely off work to aid in its promotion. Because of problems I encountered with the Wisconsin Department of Natural Resources, the discussion of the book would promote substantial sales in this state alone.

After reading this query, I instantly signed the author up. I later sold his book, retitled *Dr. Wildlife,* to Franklin Watts. The author's

Thank you very much for your consideration. I sure hope you like *Wild Patients I Have Known,* and will look forward to hearing from you.

Warm regards,

Rory C. Foster, D.V.M.

P.S.—I've just commissioned a Wisconsin wildlife artist to do a pencil sketch for the beginning of each chapter. It will take him three weeks to do the sketches.

attractive stationery had a bottom border of tiny animal silhouettes elegantly depicting several species the doctor has worked with.

ILLUSTRATION 8-2: Covering Letter

LISA COLLIER COOL
[address and phone number]

[date]

Ms. Jean Fredette
Writer's Digest Books
9933 Alliance Road
Cincinnati, OH 45242

Dear Ms. Fredette:

Enclosed is a query describing a book I'd like to write, *How to Write Irresistible Query Letters,* which I envision as fitting into your Writer's Basic Bookshelf line.

As an example of my writing on query letters, I am enclosing a copy of a piece I wrote on the subject for *Writer's Digest* magazine.

Sincerely yours,

Lisa Collier Cool

The letter in Illustration 8-2 is the actual cover letter I used when submitting the query that sold this book. To show this publisher that I am familiar with its list, I've mentioned that my book might be a good candidate for a specific line of books it is publishing.

The next query, in Illustration 8-3, has produced two offers so far, from an American publisher and a British one, and two other publishers have expressed strong interest. The exact price is being negotiated.

As with magazine queries, your book query should have your name, address, and phone number typed at the upper right of the first page. If your query is four pages or longer, a title page can be used instead.

ILLUSTRATION 8-3: Separate Book Query

Lisa Collier Cool
Street Address
City, State 00000
(000)000-0000

HOW TO GIVE GOOD PHONE

Telephone Tactics to Raise Your Power, Profits, and Performance

by
Lisa Collier Cool

Whether it's a black rotary-dial phone or a high-tech telecommunications network, the telephone is *the* essential business tool. At the touch of a finger, it can connect you to any one of a billion other phone users, giving you instant access to customers, potential employers, and other important contacts anywhere on the globe. Used skillfully, the telephone can become the instrument of your success as you save time, increase profits, and create a winning impression of yourself with people who can speed your professional advancement. Since telephone talk is not cheap—the average person spends one whole year of his or her life on the phone (8,760 hours), paying nearly $50,000 for those calls—there's an urgent need for powerful, profitable telephone techniques.

How to Give Good Phone will be a total guide to telephone success, with step-by-step programs, anecdotes and examples, and quotes from successful businessmen and women.

My book will be organized as follows:

Part 1: Power. Developing a winning telephone personality.

Chapter 1. "The Image of Success." How to analyze your telephone style and shape it into a positive telephone personality, making both your good *and* bad points work in your favor.

Chapter 2. "One Minute Phone Management." Scrutinizing your telephone "traffic flow" to maximize profitable calling, while reducing unproductive calls. Call-screening procedures.

Chapter 3. "Power Phoning." Ploys to elevate your phone status and self-defense against the power player on the other end of the line.

Chapter 4. "Let Me Speak to the Boss, Honey." Telephone tactics for women. How to avoid being mistaken for a secretary. Eliminating "female" speech patterns that may work against you.

Chapter 5. "Avoiding Telephone Hang-ups." Eliminating phonophobia and its reverse—telephonitis—and developing telephone confidence. How to sound like a winner by controlling your voice, eliminating annoying telephone habits, and using strategic pauses.

Part 2: Profits. Practical strategies for business calls.

Chapter 6. "Dialing for Dollars." Detailed analysis and advice from experts on sales strategies. The three ingredients of an effective sales pitch—and how to deliver them.

Chapter 7. "Selling Yourself." Creating the right impression on potential employers, prospective customers, and powerful new contacts. Attention-grabbing openers.

Chapter 8. "The Bottom Line." Sales tactics to get higher prices and better negotiating conditions. Recognizing different types of buyers and adapting your pitch appropriately.

Chapter 9. "Getting Better Buys." Analyzing the different kinds of sellers. Picking up underlying messages that get you price concessions and favorable negotiating conditions.

Chapter 10. "The Price is Right." How to use the phone as a negotiating weapon. Overcoming the tactics of intimidation. Closing the deal.

Chapter 11. "The Check is in the Mail." The fine art of creative complaining. How to get prompt action.

Chapter 12. "Getting Off the Hook." Dealing with crisis calls, complaints, angry callers, bad news, and awkward situations.

Part 3: Performance. Getting the most from your phone.

Chapter 13. "Electronic Rendezvous." Conducting meetings and presentations using conference calls and speakerphones.

Chapter 14. "High-Tech Networking." Getting on line with your computer to amass information, make business connections, speed purchasing. Electronic banking and mail.

Chapter 15. "The Telephone and the Law." Legalities for the phone user. Follow-up to telephone deals.

Chapter 16. "Cheaper Talk." A guide to telephone equipment.

Chapter 17. "Total Telephone Success." A powerhouse of advanced phonesmanship techniques for the expert.

I envision strong interest in *How to Give Good Phone.* Effective telephone communication is vital to the successful executive, as well as the ambitious newcomer to business and the job applicant. Secretaries and assistants will find the recommendations on procedures and etiquette valuable reading, while those who make their living on the phone will find hundreds of tested strategies to increase profits and cut costs.

The book will contain seventy thousand words and can be written in six months. I am highly qualified to write this book. As a literary agent of twelve years' standing, representing highly successful and best-selling writers, I have extensive experience with the telephone techniques I'll be describing. As a writer whose work has reached more than six million readers, I can offer the book's buyer a good read, as well as an informative one.

I am the author of two books: *How to Sell Every Magazine Article You Write* (Writer's Digest Books, Fall 1986; first serial rights to *Writer's Digest* magazine) and *How to Write Irresistible Query Letters* (Writer's Digest, Spring 1987).

My magazine credits include articles for *Family Circle, Publishers Weekly, Penthouse, Harper's Magazine, Glamour, Cosmopolitan, Playgirl, Modern Bride,* and about twenty other magazines and newspapers. I also am a former faculty member of Parson's School of Design, teaching "Magazine Writing" and "Fiction/Nonfiction Workshop." I have appeared on television in connection with my writing and am willing to promote my book vigorously on radio and television.

Chapter 9

A Rogue's Gallery

Watch out! You may be undermining the effectiveness of your book or article query—or worse still, making an amateurish impression—with subtle mistakes. Having received perhaps ten thousand queries during my years as an agent, I've identified a variety of common flaws that could be working against you. Here's my "least wanted" list:

Moniker Mishaps.   Few mistakes arouse an editor's ire more than spelling his or her name incorrectly. I've frequently received letters rendering my first name as "Liza" or "Leslie," and was once addressed as "Shirley" by a particularly confused writer. Another unfortunately memorable query opened with the salutation "Dear Agent Collies."

Using outdated directories can also make a poor impression—if your letter arrives at all—since an obsolete address speaks poorly of your research skills. Similarly, addressing your query to an editor or agent who's long since departed from the company is sloppy and often delays response considerably. It's wise to double-check the names and addresses you find in current directories with a phone call to the firm.

Format Fumbles.   Although the two formats I've recommended are not the only acceptable approaches—a couple of my most successful clients prefer to format their queries as memos, for example—extreme variations are likely to signal to an editor that the query is the work of an amateur.

I've often heard editors complain of receiving *handwritten* queries and material typed so faintly that it's hard to read. Offbeat stationery and unusual typefaces or ink colors (remember that black is the only acceptable ink color) also work against you. Making your query *look* like a winner is important; make sure your type is crisp and leave wide margins for easier reading.

Horn Tooting. Editors do expect a bit of sell, but avoid tooting your own horn *too* loudly. Describing your idea as "the story of the century" or "a surefire best-seller" is definitely overkill. A really good story will practically sell itself, and a weaker one needs buttressing with solid, factual information rather than outlandish claims that will just turn the editor off.

Attention-getting devices tend to backfire, as do most attempts at humor. I've received several queries from male authors beginning, "Dear Lisa, I'd like to propose to you." My reaction was somewhat like that of Queen Victoria—"We were not amused"—especially the tenth time around.

Terms of Indecision. Don't go to the other extreme, however, and let modest or self-effacing remarks create a negative impression. An editor wants to buy from writers who believe in their own work, so you should avoid even the slightest suggestion of doubt. Here are some examples of negative phrasing I've culled from queries I've received; don't let them creep into your query.

- *The book [or article] would . . .* The use of the conditional tense subtly suggests a lack of confidence in your idea. Always say, "The book [or article] *will* . . ." to imply that you consider its publication a certainty.

- *I'll welcome your editorial input.* Bad because it sounds as though you'll *need* editing. Surprising as it may seem, many of today's book and magazine editors prefer to do as little editing as possible. The days when an editor would spend six months helping an author rewrite his or her book are long gone. With the increased volume of titles turned out each year, editors lack the time to provide in-depth attention to each work. This is equally true in the magazine business, where the fast-paced schedule of putting out a monthly or weekly publication leaves minimal time for editing. Instead, editors want material that is essentially publishable as delivered.

- *I know there are a lot of other books/articles on the topic.* Why offer an editor a ready-made reason for rejection? Rephrase as "My book differs from others in the field because . . ." or "My article will be the first to explain. . . ."

- *I'm an unpublished author.* Work on creating a strong bio emphasizing your *other* qualifications—don't draw attention to your lack of publishing credits.

- *I've written six other books/articles, but this is the first one I consider worthy of publication.* The suggestion that you have a hoard of unpublished works that you consider to be of inferior quality strikes terror into an editor's heart as she envisions your query being followed by a deluge of unpromising material. Avoid referring to other works you've written unless they are either published or presented in your query as candidates for publication.

Autobiographical Remarks. A surprising number of writers preface their queries with long explanations of how they happened to think of the idea: "When I was a student at Nondescript U., I was interested in psychology. Putting this interest aside, I spent thirty years as an accountant, and now that retirement looms. . " Unless you're proposing an autobiography or personal experience project, skip the life story and just tell the editor or agent your idea.

Fuzzy Thinking. If an editor or agent can't understand your idea, he or she won't buy it. Make sure your basic topic and slant are clearly stated in either the first or second paragraph of the query, and that you've selected a title that reveals both your subject and slant.

The material that follows your statement of purpose should be organized to smoothly develop your idea. Avoid abrupt shifts in subject; you don't want to have an editor who is reading along to suddenly look up and say, "Huh?" Once the editor's interest has been disrupted this way, you've probably lost the sale.

Unless you are dealing with a university press or specialty magazine, it's wise to assume that the editor's knowledge of the topic is comparable to that of a reasonably informed layperson. If your subject is a bit esoteric, make sure you define technical terms and describe new concepts in easy-to-understand language. It's better to *slightly* underestimate the intelligence of the editor than to confuse him with unfamiliar material.

Test the query on a few friends—but avoid the temptation to explain it to them before they read; you won't be at the editor's office to provide elaboration. Have the test audience read the material, then quiz them on their understanding of the subject.

Faulty Facts.   One of my clients lost a sale because he misidentified one of the personalities he was discussing in the query. The editor noticed the mistake and concluded that the author was a poor researcher. Relying on memory can result in similar errors. To be safe, recheck each fact, even if you are already certain you have the correct information.

Realize too that not all research sources are equally reliable. Another writer I know gathered information from articles published by a certain activist group. Unfortunately for him, this group's newsletter contained several key errors which my client unwittingly repeated in his query—costing him the opportunity to make a large sale.

Stylistic Stumbles.   Even the most meticulous writer can compose an unfortunately worded sentence or spoil a well crafted phrase with a typo that obscures meaning. Worst of all, such mistakes can create unintentional humor, as in the letter I once received concerning a work entitled "The Joy of Sobriety" which rendered the title as "The *Job* of Sobriety."

If you're using a word processor, it's easy to go astray by positioning deletions, insertions, and rearranged text incorrectly. In rechecking a recent query before submission, I noticed that one of my sentences was missing several key words, rendering it nonsensical. Make sure your copy does compute by reviewing the final printout before mailing. Check the editor's name, publication, and address for typos, too.

The Query That Just Won't Quit.   The longer your query is, the greater your risk of boring the editor. The ideal query has just enough information to spark a sale—and *not one word more.* If your article query exceeds two pages, or your book query five pages, odds are that cuts are indicated. Eliminate minor points, wordy phrases, excessive adjectives and adverbs, and other space-wasters—a sound strategy for any query, regardless of starting length.

Lack of SASE. All submissions to agents and editors (both book and magazine) should be accompanied by a self-addressed, stamped envelope for the return of the material or the editor's reply. Be sure your return envelope is large enough to hold your material. (Use a No. 10 business envelope for short queries; a nine-by-twelve-inch manila envelope for long queries or finished articles.) Editors find it annoying having to refold queries in origami-like shapes to fit into some undersized envelope.

Even when you become better established as a writer, it's wise to include an SASE in all communications with magazine and book editors and literary agents. However, most agents won't expect you to send an SASE with correspondence or submissions once they've accepted you as a client. The same is true of editors: usually after an editor has bought one or more articles from you, you can omit the SASE in future submissions to that particular editor.

Don't attach cash or a check in lieu of the SASE or ask the editor or agent to return your material some unusual way, such as by private courier.

Market Misjudgments. Before submitting to a book publisher, study its latest catalog (the publisher will usually send you one free on request) to make sure your idea fits the house's "personality." A publisher specializing in literary fiction and serious nonfiction, like Alfred A. Knopf, isn't a good bet for your book on *Breakdancing*.

Studying the current catalog is also helpful in giving your cover letter or letter query a personal touch, because you can mention any connections between your book and works now on the list. For paperback publishers, you may also want to check out "dump" displays at your book store, where the publisher will have several of its more popular titles grouped in cardboard stands near the front of the store.

Market directories are also helpful in determining what book and magazine publishers want. *Writer's Market*, for example, is an annual publication with detailed listings of more than 4,000 paying markets for books and articles, as well as other kinds of writing.

Since editors and agents receive such a heavy volume of submissions, take every possible step to "rejectionproof" your query. Most queries are first read by editorial assistants, who are frequently given total discretion in rejecting queries. If a superficial inspection reveals an obvious flaw of some sort, you can't count on the benefit of the doubt—rejection is the most likely outcome.

By sidestepping the common pitfalls—and adding strong selling points—you will make your query part of the elite group of ideas that is seriously considered for publication. Though some publishers may turn you down for reasons beyond your control (such as lack of success with other books in the subject area or an article on the same topic already scheduled for future publication), a query that couples a professional approach with a sound idea can easily launch your writing career—or build upon the successes you've already had.

Chapter 10

Strategic Submissions

Once your query is finished, the alchemy of salesmanship can transform your idea into income. All it takes to sell your query is to locate just *one* editor who likes the idea enough to buy it. With the right submission strategy, that editor could be just one postage stamp away—I know several freelancers who've sold their first time out. Or you may find, as another writer I know did, that sheer persistence is the key. This particular author endured fifty-six rejections of his first book but found the pot of gold at the end of submission rainbow on his fifty-seventh submission. The book went on to make more than sixty thousand dollars in royalties.

Having sold more than five hundred books as an agent and one hundred or so of my own articles, I've developed some submission strategies that will help you get the fastest possible results and ensure that you don't inadvertently sell your work too cheaply by missing the best markets, a common error of inexperienced authors.

Know the Markets. I'm often accosted by would-be authors at cocktail parties and asked if some article idea would be right for *Esquire* or *The New Yorker*. Ninety-nine percent of the time, I have to inform the aspiring author that the topic is totally inappropriate for either of these publications—as he or she could have easily determined by actually *reading* an issue or two. Or these cocktail clients, as I call them, are convinced that their guide to Texas restaurants is just what Simon & Schuster's list needs—never realizing that a regional publisher like Texas Monthly Press would be a much better submission bet.

Knowledge of the marketplace is an agent's stock in trade, but you can easily acquire the same information on your own by devoting an hour or two a week to market study—homework that will quickly pay off in increased sales opportunities.

The first step is to consult a good publishing directory: *Writer's Handbook* (The Writer Inc.) and *Writer's Market* (Writer's Digest Books) are two of the most popular. Both are updated annually and can be found in most libraries or at your bookstore. Since *Writer's Market* has the greater number of market listings—four thousand versus twenty-five hundred for *Writer's Handbook*—I consider it a better buy for home use.

To use *Writer's Market*, simply scan the table of contents and ask yourself, "Would my article appeal to animal magazines? Art magazines? Association, club, and fraternal publications . . . ?" When you locate a likely category, such as "women's," turn to the actual listings and learn specifics about each of the twenty or so magazines in this category. Each listing (book publishers are also included) contains the publisher's address, the editor you should submit to, type of material currently sought, prices paid, and various submission tips.

These listings will help you prepare a preliminary submission list for your query. For additional market ideas, subscribe to *Writer's Digest* magazine and/or *The Writer*, which have monthly coverage of new publications, changes in direction or staff at existing magazines and book publishers, and helpful tips on writing and submitting your work.

After you've identified likely markets for your article idea, read at least one issue of each magazine on your submission list. Some of these will be available at the library; sample copies of others can be purchased through the magazine, at large newsstands, or at backdate magazine stores. Study the entire magazine, looking at *the ads* (they'll help you visualize the reader by suggesting his or her probable level of income, lifestyle, and marital status); *the letters to the editor and "in the next issue" announcements* (which clue you into topics covered in previous and upcoming issues); *the editor's page* (which helps you understand the "personality" of the publication as perceived by its leadership); and *the masthead* (which will offer you a selection of editors to submit to and the address of the magazine).

Naturally, *the articles* will be the most instructive of all: use them to pinpoint the correct *length* (one printed page of text without ads usually corresponds to 1,000 words), *format* (lots of how-to pieces suggest that your query should propose a similarly organized piece, for example), *style* (if the tone is chatty, your query could echo this preference), and *topic* (the presence of one medical piece implies that others might be bought in the future).

To increase your market awareness, make a point of reading two or three new magazines each week, in addition to those on current submission lists. It's best to direct your queries to magazines that you personally enjoy reading; the right style and subjects will come more naturally to you. And exposure to so many articles will trigger new ideas for future queries as you react to your reading. Short of time? Substitute magazine reading for TV viewing and you'll soon have a huge reservoir of market information at your fingertips.

MAGAZINE QUERY SUBMISSIONS

To fine-tune your submission approach, try these strategies:

Don't Overlook the Obvious.   Some authors outsmart themselves by dreaming up elaborate sales points to use on unlikely markets while neglecting a more promising group of magazines. To decide which magazines are the best bets, try summarizing your article into key words. Let's say you've written a query for a profile article of a young woman who bought and renovated a brownstone in New York City. Key words might be *young woman, brownstone renovation,* and *New York.* Thus your best markets are women's magazines, home and architectural publications, regional and local magazines for New Yorkers, and area newspapers or Sunday supplements.

Submit to the Right Editor.   For the fastest results, make sure you are sending the query to the right person at the magazine. Never address a submission to "articles editor" or "the editors." Instead, do a little detective work and learn the *name* of the articles editor. Frequently there will be someone identified by this title on the magazine's masthead; if not, submissions can be sent to one of the senior editors, the managing editor, or specialized editors, such as "health editor," that match the general category your article falls into. If you're having trouble deciding which editor to submit to, call the magazine for further guidance.

Don't submit to the editor listed at the top of the masthead. Except at very small magazines, the top editor is generally more of an executive than an acquiring editor. "Contributing editors" are also a poor bet; these are freelance writers who work frequently for the magazine.

Start at the Top. If there's one magazine on your list that pays $750, another that pays $400, and six others that pay $150, the wrong order of submissions could cost you up to $600 in lost income. Always go for the best possible market *first*. While the best-paying markets tend to be the most competitive and therefore harder to sell to, don't let a prestigious reputation scare you off. If careful market study has you convinced that *Esquire* or *The New Yorker* really is a good prospect, send the query out. I know a number of writers who've sold their very first article to major national magazines— and there's no reason why you can't do the same with the right idea.

Try Every Prospect. No one likes to receive rejection after rejection, but some queries are harder to sell than others. Unless several editors—not just one or two—detect some fatal flaw in the idea, continue submitting until you've tried every single publication on your list.

Even when the prospects seem exhausted, *don t quit*. Unless your idea becomes dated, keep alert for announcements of new magazines in the field; look for news developments that could signal an upswing in interest; and, if all else fails, wait a couple of years, change the title, rewrite it a bit, and send it to the same magazine *again*, submitting to a different editor. After my query was rejected by one editor at a particular publication, I used this approach two years later and got a five-hundred-dollar assignment from another editor at the same magazine.

Profit from Rejection. If any of your rejection letters seem halfway encouraging or contain specific criticisms, consider it an invitation to submit new ideas. Editors aren't in the business of raising false hopes; if one says, "Try me with other projects," get some new queries out promptly. If a concrete objection is raised, consider sending a revised query that counters the criticism. Even a lukewarm response shows *some* interest. A different idea may kindle the spark enough to produce a sale.

Play the Numbers Game. The more ideas you send out, the more likely you are to sell some of them. One writer I know sent ten queries to a magazine she wanted to write for, and over the next two years she received assignments for all ten of them. Another author sent six ideas to a teen publication and was rewarded with a six-hundred-dollar assignment—oddly enough for the idea she had considered *least* promising. Some magazines don't like to receive so many submissions at once from a writer; to play it safe, just send two or three ideas in each submission. You can always send more after you have the response to the first batch.

When an editor *asks* you for more ideas, however, send several of your best queries. This request indicates strong interest. (See chapter 7 for multiple-query formats.) Keep your production high by sending out at least one new query each week—write more if you have the time.

BOOK QUERY SUBMISSIONS

To decide which book publishers might be best for your query, consult *Writer's Market, Writer's Handbook,* or *Literary Market Place* (available at most libraries) to see which houses publish nonfiction books in the general category you've selected. Also, ask your librarian to let you look at the large "spring announcement" and "fall announcement" issues of *Publishers Weekly,* the trade magazine of book publishing, which will contain extensive advertising and listings of the current season's crop of titles. This is helpful because you'll see what kind of books dozens of publishers are emphasizing, to get a better picture of whose list would be appropriate for your book.

Once you've assembled your submission list, check the personnel listings in *Literary Market Place* and *Writer's Market* for the names of editors and senior editors at that publisher. Any of these will probably be okay for your submission; if it doesn't interest the editor you've sent it to, chances are that he or she will pass it along to the right coworker. Better still, telephone the assistant of one of these editors (*not* the senior editor or editor-in-chief) for further guidance. Ask him or her, "Who handles most of your sports [or whichever subject area your book falls into] books?" and direct your query to the editor specified.

MULTIPLE SUBMISSIONS

Although multiple submissions (or "simultaneous submissions," as they are sometimes called) are considered quite acceptable in book publishing and for submissions to agents, magazine publishers are still a bit resistant to the idea. With book publishers and agents, identify your submission as a simultaneous offering by stating at the end of your cover letter, "I am also showing this to a few other publishers" (or agents, as the case might be).

For magazine submissions, however, my practice is to avoid raising editorial hackles with any reference to a multiple submission. Instead, I just use the same covering letter or letter query that I'd use for a single submission. Several writers and agents I know use the same tactic to avoid creating a negative psychological climate.

But what if more than one magazine should offer to buy the piece? Though it's never happened to me in thirteen years of such "covert" multiple submissions, I have decided that if it did, I'd do one of two things. If the two markets were noncompeting (that is, didn't overlap in circulation), I'd simply write two *different* articles. If this were impossible—say *Mademoiselle* and *Glamour* both offered to buy the same idea—I'd sell it to the highest bidder and decline the other offer.

You may be wondering if the rejected editor would then refuse to buy your future article ideas out of spite. From my experience as an agent, I've discovered that the reverse is true. An editor who fails to land a project becomes *more* eager to buy the next time around, feeling that this author must be very hot to attract so many offers. In the heat of the moment, a rejected editor will sometimes make some stinging remarks out of annoyance, but these tempests inevitably blow over by the next morning.

If you'd rather make multiple submissions overtly, the best approach is to compile a submission list composed exclusively of publications that announce no objection to multiple submissions in either *Writer's Market* or their writer's guidelines. To make the revelation as discreetly as possible, type "simultaneous submission" at the lower left of the cover letter or letter query you are sending.

SENDING YOUR SUBMISSION OUT

Whether you are sending a single or multiple submission to magazine or book publishers, your first step is to type the material in crisp, dark lettering, making sure to include your name, address, and daytime phone number on both the cover letter (if used) and query. If you are using a letter query—which is better for single submissions—make one photocopy for your files or use carbon paper when typing the final copy. For cover letter and query combos, make as many copies of the *query* (*not* the cover letter) as you have names on your submission list, plus one spare for your files.

When submitting queries that will be accompanied by cover letters, always send a photocopy of the query and keep the original at home—even if you are making single submissions. Editors may lose or damage your query, but if you have the original, you can simply make a fresh photocopy for new submissions, avoiding the necessity of retyping the entire query. Virtually every magazine editor in the business is willing to consider photocopied queries these days.

For your cover letter, however, *always* type an individual letter for each editor you are submitting to. Do not try to save time by photocopying the text of the letter and adding the heading and salutation in the same type. Editors have eagle eyes for this trick and dislike the impersonality of such correspondence. Letter queries should also be individually typed. Letters typed on word processing computers are also acceptable to most publications.

To mail your queries, either fold them in thirds and place them in a No. 10 business envelope (best for queries of four pages or less) or mail them unfolded in a nine-by-twelve manila envelope (best for longer queries). Make sure to include a self-addressed, stamped envelope for the return of the query. The most economical way to mail a query is first class mail. If you would like to be notified of its arrival, for a modest additional charge you can send it "return receipt requested."

SUBMISSION CHECKLIST

Before sending your query out, look it over one last time and make sure that:

- The query is free of grammatical or typographic errors.

- The editor's name, title, address, and magazine or publisher are correct.

- Your name, address, and daytime phone number appear on *both* the cover letter and attached query.

- You've included a self-addressed, stamped envelope with each submission.

- You've matched the correct cover letter with the correct envelope for each of your multiple submissions.

- You've got a clear photocopy of everything you're submitting.

- You've made a record of where each submission is going.

- Your return address is on both the outside envelope and the SASE.

- You've put the correct postage on each submission and attached a return receipt (optional).

WAITING FOR RESULTS

At least half the editors you deal with will be quite slow to respond. Typically, the fastest replies are rejections; acceptances tend to take a bit longer. Consult *Writer's Market* and the magazine or publisher's own writer's guidelines for the length of time the company usually takes to respond to queries—usually four to eight weeks.

If the specified time period passes without a response, wait two more weeks, then send a tactful reminder. If any new developments in the news suggest that your idea is even more saleable, add these new sales points to your reminder. Otherwise, say something like,

"Because ten weeks have passed since I submitted my query [give title], I thought it was a good time to inquire how the submission is faring with you." If the magazine or publishing house is nearby, you may wish to telephone the editor's assistant—*not* the editor—to check on progress.

Some writers worry that even this gentle nudge will prompt an editor to reject their material. However, rest assured that your reminder will only speed results—whether a rejection or a sale. If your first inquiry doesn't produce a response, send another note two or three weeks later. If you hear nothing for three months, consider telephoning. Your editor may have left the organization, leaving your query in a pile of "slush," as unsolicited material is called in publishing. Or the query may have been lost.

DO EDITORS STEAL IDEAS?

You may also be worrying that an editor will steal your idea and assign it to a better known writer. While it's impossible to assure you that this never happens, I believe it's highly unlikely. Most often when a writer thinks his idea has been stolen, it turns out that the idea is a rather commonplace one, such as "How to Have a Garage Sale." An editor at a major woman's magazine told me that this particular idea has been submitted to her dozens of times by different authors. If she ever runs an article on the topic, no doubt all the other authors will be hollering, "Thief!"

Furthermore, most magazines and book publishers have no reason to steal your ideas. They receive hundreds of excellent ideas that have to be rejected for lack of room. When ideas are that easy to come by, why risk expensive lawsuits by stealing them?

SOLD! ARTICLE CONTRACTS

If your article query strikes an editor as a likely candidate for acquisition, expect one of two possible outcomes. If you don't have many credits, chances are that you'll be asked to write the piece "on speculation," meaning that the magazine makes no guarantee that it will actually buy the finished piece. Since most magazines work this way with inexperienced authors, writing "on spec" is a sensible move for a beginner. Before embarking on the piece, ask the editor what fee you might expect for an acceptable article, how long the piece should be, and when the editor would like to receive it. Then send a comfirming letter like the one in Illustration 10-1.

If you have several previous credits or a particularly exciting idea, many magazines will *commission* the article through an assignment letter, contract, or oral discussion. A typical agreement will specify both the fee to be paid if the piece is accepted and a lesser fee to be paid if it's rejected (the "kill fee" or "write-off fee," in publishing parlance). The agreement should also indicate the deadline for delivery of the article, the number of words desired, and which rights the magazine wishes to acquire. If the terms are set orally, send a confirming letter for the editor to sign and return: Send two copies of the letter, one for the editor to keep for the magazine's files, one for him or her to sign and return to you.

ILLUSTRATION 10-1: Confirming Letter for Writing "On Spec"

YOUR NAME
Address

Date

Ms. Judicia S. Pruning
Editor
Regional Magazine
29 Publisher's Row
City, State 00000

Dear Ms. Pruning:

I'm delighted that you want me to write [give title] on speculation. I will deliver a piece of 2,000 words by [deadline], and I understand you will pay $350 if you find the piece to be publishable.

Sincerely yours,

Your Name

ILLUSTRATION 10-2: Confirming Letter for Writing on Contract

YOUR NAME
Address

Date

Ms. Judicia S. Pruning
Editor
Regional Magazine
29 Publisher's Row
City, State 00000

Dear Ms. Pruning:

To confirm our oral discussion of [exact date], we have agreed that I will write an article of [number of words] for your publication. The fee will be [price], payable upon [acceptance/number of days after acceptance/publication] for [specify rights acquired]. Should the article be rejected, you will pay a kill fee of [15 percent/20 percent/25 percent or whatever]. I will deliver the article on [delivery date].

Please confirm your agreement by signing and returning the attached copy of this letter.

Sincerely yours,

Your Name

_____

Signed and agreed,
Judicia S. Pruning
for Regional Magazine

KNOWING YOUR RIGHTS

Here's a brief guide to the most commonly bought rights, with a capsule definition of each:

Work Made for Hire. This agreement transfers every possible right, including your copyright, to the buyer. It is considered the least desirable contract; you should accept it as a last resort for the right price.

All Rights. This gives the magazine every conceivable right to your article, except copyright, for thirty-five years. After that, you own all the rights again.

All Publishing Rights. You own the movie, TV, video, and other dramatic rights, and the magazine owns all publishing rights throughout the world.

All Periodical Rights. You own dramatic and book rights, the magazine owns all magazine and newspaper publishing rights throughout the world.

English-Language Serial Rights. The publisher owns the right to publish or license others to publish the work in magazines and newspapers printed in the English language. You own the right to license translations to foreign-language publications, as well as all book and dramatic rights.

North American English-Language Serial Rights. The publishers' rights apply only to publication in U.S. and Canadian magazines and newspapers.

First North American English-Language Rights, One-Time Use Only. The magazine has the right to publish the article once, prior to any other publication of the piece, in the United States and Canada. You are free to resell the article to other magazines and to newspapers, here and abroad. This is considered the most desirable contract.

Second Serial Rights. This refers to the right to republish a previously published piece. It refers to reselling a previously published article or excerpts from a published book. There's no limit to how many second serial (or reprint, as it's sometimes called) sales you can make of the same article.

ARTICLE FEES

Magazine rates are quite variable. Some small magazines pay nothing but a few "contributor's copies," others have starting rates as high as three thousand dollars or more. The minimum rates for articles for a specific publication are usually listed in the *Writer's Market* entry for that publication or may appear in the magazine's own writer's guidelines.

The exact rate you'll be offered depends on such factors as the length of the article, your previous publishing background, the importance of the subject, and the circulation of the magazine. Some magazines also pay expenses.

Small magazines usually pay $5 to $350; medium-sized ones, $250 to $750; and major magazines, $500 to $3,000. Most magazines will give you a raise once you've written one or two articles for them.

BOOK CONTRACTS

Book contracts are highly complex documents. For a detailed explanation of a typical trade book agreement and further information on magazine contracts, see *How to Understand and Negotiate a Book Contract or Magazine Agreement*, by Richard Balkin (Writer's Digest Books).

If a book publisher wants your book, you'll be offered an *advance against royalties*, which might be in the range of $2,000 to $15,000 for a typical first nonfiction book, though higher advances are sometimes paid. For a book that has not yet been written, expect to receive part of your advance upon signing the contract, the rest when you deliver a satisfactory book. Some contracts call for payment in three, four, or five installments.

After the book is published, you will earn a royalty on each copy sold; your advance will be deducted from these royalties. Hardcover publishers usually pay royalties of 10 percent of the list price on the first 5,000 to 7,500 copies sold, 12½ percent on the next 5,000 to 7,500 copies sold, and 15 percent thereafter. Paperback publishers have variable royalty scales, but often pay 6 percent on the first 150,000 copies sold and 8 percent thereafter.

CONTRACTS WITH AGENTS

Many agents do not use a written contract; others do have a one- or two-page agreement with clients. Almost half of literary agents now charge a 15 percent commission; the rest charge 10 percent. This commission is deducted from all earnings on each book the agent places during the period of representation, and it survives after the termination of representation. Some agents have contracts providing for a minimum period of representation, such as a year; others use open-ended agreements.

Most agents charge the author nothing unless they actually place a book or article for the person, although a few charge "reading fees" to unpublished authors. These fees can range from nominal ($20 to $50) up to several hundred dollars. To find agents, consult *Guide to Literary Agents & Art/Photo Reps*, which lists both fee-charging and non-fee-charging agents.

LOOK BEFORE YOU SIGN

Whether your contract is with an agent, book publisher, or magazine, read it carefully, *even* if you plan to have a lawyer look at it too. For most magazine or agency contracts, a lawyer is unnecessary, but for unagented book contracts, a legal review is helpful for the first-time author. For free legal advice—available only for authors of modest income—contact the Volunteer Lawyers for the Arts, which has about 30 offices scattered over the country. The New York City branch is at 1285 Avenue of the Americas, New York, NY 10019, (212) 977-9270.

Unless this is your very first sale, try a little negotiation. Frequently you can extract a slightly higher price or better terms simply by asking. If you're turned down, you've still accomplished something by creating a favorable climate for the *next* contract by letting your publisher know that you're a businesslike type, not a starry-eyed beginner who'll grab the first deal the publisher puts on the table.

While it's a tactical error to press too hard, a mildly assertive approach can really pay off, I've discovered. Over the past two years, I've more than *doubled* my writing income, not by increasing output but by asking for a raise every single time I sell something. Remember that you have to *ask* to receive, and you could reap similar bonanzas from your queries!

Chapter 11

Anatomy of a Winner

As a writer, you would, of course, like to start selling consistently, get bigger prices for your articles, and establish a profitable freelance career. In this chapter I've collected successful queries from a variety of writers to illustrate the techniques that produce results. You'll see the actual text of the query, as well as the price and market it sold to, along with my commentary on the query.

As you look them over, you'll probably be struck by the variety of styles and approaches that work. There's plenty of room for creativity in structuring your own queries; as you write them, you'll undoubtedly discover a literary "voice" that feels natural for you. Some writers develop a winning formula and use it for all their queries. Others prefer to let their subject and market dictate the correct approach.

What all these queries have in common is three basic elements: a lead that gets attention, a compelling description of the idea, and an authoritative author's bio. (Omit the bio for new submissions to markets that have already bought your work.) Like master chefs, these authors have taken these ingredients and blended them into tasty new concoctions. So can you!

BOOK QUERY TO AN AGENT

The query by Catherine Lilly and Daniel Martin, shown in Illustration 11-1 on page 115, struck me as an intriguing presentation of an abstract subject. Oscar Collier, the agent who handled the work, sold the book to Taylor Publishing (1987 publication). Excerpts appeared in *Self* magazine. The authors have asked me to omit the price.

I also like the way the bios of the two collaborators were presented. The layout calls attention to the strong qualifications of the two authors.

ARTICLE QUERIES

The query in Illustration 11-2, on page 118, resulted in a $500 sale. It's a good example of how to sell to regional magazines. In the first sentence, William Hoffman clearly states that his profile subject is a resident of the area served by the publication, an important point to this particular publication.

The use of gambler's argot—*crossroader*, for example—is a nice, professional touch. It shows the editor that Hoffman has done his homework by intimately familiarizing himself with his subject.

A final selling point is the description of Soares as a sort of modern-day Robin Hood, since it shows the slant—that the profile subject is a heroic kind of outlaw whom the reader will sympathize with.

The second article query, in Illustration 11-3, sold for three thousand dollars to a major woman's magazine (the author has requested that I keep the name of the magazine and editor confidential). The friendly, personal tone works well for two reasons. First, since Elizabeth Tener is making contact with a new editor at a publication she's previously sold to—a very common situation with the high rate of editorial turnover in the magazine world—it establishes an instant rapport. It's also appropriate to her sympathetic treatment of the subject.

She's also selected a timely topic and a good slant. Since this publication is oriented to married women with families, reader identification with the subject matter should be strong. Putting her story in the framework of a "true life" story of one particular family is an excellent way of personalizing the complex subject of drug abuse among the young.

The use of specifics enhances the query. The editor can easily see that the piece will concentrate on new solutions to an old problem, through a true success story.

The author's strategy of building on work she's done before on the subject—the article she mentions for *Young Miss*—is a valuable one. Selling more than one article on the same topic allows you to get more mileage out of your research time, raise your hourly pay rate, and build solid credentials as an "expert" on the subject.

The next query, shown in Illustration 11-4, resulted in a large sale to *Good Housekeeping* (the author has requested that I keep the exact amount confidential). It is typical of the queries used by more successful authors—very short and to the point. Despite its brevity, it has several strong selling points. First, it uses numbers—"the ten (or twenty) most common medical disorders"—which is a preferred organizing device for women's magazines. It is specific—a wide range of problems are listed.

Its unusual angle is aptly summed up by the title and reinforced by the italicizing of *experimental*. The reference to "top subspecialists" conveys both a sense of authority and a familiarity with the medical field; most writers would have used the word *specialists*, not *subspecialists*, which is the correct term in this case.

The final paragraph shows Maxine Abrams's close familiarity with this particular market through its reference to "a *Good Housekeeping* book," which is a major article of considerable length. In your dealings with any particular magazine, alert yourself to any of that publication's buzzwords an editor might use in correspondence or phone discussions. Other magazines may use different terminology; at *Cosmopolitan*, for example, such articles are called "majors," while short pieces are labeled "f.o.b.," or "front of the book" pieces, referring to their customary placement in the front of the magazine. Learning these terms will help you frame future queries along the lines the editors prefer.

If you're a starting writer, most of your queries will be longer than this, because you not only have to sell the idea, but convince the editor that you can do the job effectively. However, once an editor has bought several pieces from you, the burden of proof is no longer so heavy, and your queries can gradually become shorter and shorter.

Over the past few years, I've sent several queries to Peter Bloch at *Penthouse*. Each was returned with a cordial note, citing a specific reason why the idea didn't work—usually a competing project. Each rejection ended with a friendly suggestion to send new ideas. Finally the editor suggested an idea of his own, which turned into my breakthrough query, producing a four-thousand-dollar assignment. (See Illustration 11-5.)

There's a lesson in this you can benefit from. While even the friendliest rejection is likely to seem discouraging, often all it takes is a bit of perseverance to turn rejection into a sale. If editors are rejecting your ideas due to competing projects, this suggests that your basic idea is on target—all that's off is your timing. Showing an editor that you have a solid grasp of his readership by submitting appropriate ideas will eventually pay off. Sooner or later you'll hit the magic moment and get your query there *first*.

If an editor sends back one of your ideas with a suggestion to submit new ideas, follow up immediately. This kind of encouragement is always sincere and proves that your style and approach are effective, even if the particular idea you've sent hasn't worked out for that editor. A perfectly good idea may be rejected for such reasons as a heavy inventory in that particular article category, excessive inventory in all areas, editorial quirks peculiar to that individual publication, or other factors beyond your control.

When an editor makes you a present of one of his or her own ideas, as has happened to me several times, you're more than halfway to a sale. Seize the moment—editors are fickle creatures and the idea's appeal may fade if you don't respond quickly. Take extra pains to supply first-rate research and an alluring presentation. Such opportunities are seldom repeated if you don't do a bang-up job the first time around.

One final pointer: be sure to remind the editor that the idea originated with him. He'll appreciate being given credit and will be favorably disposed to the idea; after all it was his in the first place!

The fifth article query, shown on page 123, resulted in the author's first magazine sale, a one-thousand-dollar assignment from *Audubon,* one of the more difficult nature markets to crack. The author has turned his professional expertise into a powerful selling point—the entire query rings with authority. This effect is derived from the extensive use of firsthand anecdotes from Robert Elgin's own experience, as well as the frequent references to the experts within the field to whom he has personal access.

The success of the query is also a result of Elgin's having identified a widespread pattern of abuse that relatively few people outside the field are aware of. The readers of this publication are likely to be outraged by the article—which could have the beneficial effect of inspiring greater regulation in this area. Editors like to get involved in deserving causes like this.

This query was written for agented submission, so is not addressed to the *Audubon* editor but to the agent, whose name and address have been omitted at her request.

Susan Lapinski's query for a human interest article, Illustration 11-7, produced a sale to *Parade* magazine, a national newspaper supplement, for $2,500. It was accompanied by a short covering letter.

The query's success demonstrates how a writer's reading can lead to good sales. The author saw an item that interested her on page 1 of *The New York Times* and immediately proposed an article on the subject to a likely market—this newspaper supplement. "I'm amazed that no one else seems to have sold a piece on this," Susan Lapinski says. "When I saw it on the front page of the *Times*, I thought people would be jumping all over the story."

Lapinski points out that using ideas gleaned from the newspaper saves research time. "All the basic facts for my query were already in the *Times* piece. All I had to do was write it up and send it off."

The bio has been omitted because this is the author's second sale to *Parade.* Her credits include a book and sales to several major magazines.

Following the last line of the query, you'll see "(30)," which is standard newspaperese for "the end." I thought this was a good psychological touch, in that it suggests that the author is experienced in the ways of newspaper writing—which would make a favorable impression on the editors of a magazine distributed through newspapers.

ILLUSTRATION 11-1: Catherine Lilly and Daniel Martin

Dear Agent:

We've written a book entitled *Unlocking Opportunity: Tools for Living in Today's Uncertain Times.* It deals with the role of chance in daily life, with insights from literature and modern science. We would like your help in getting published. It is approximately 110,000 words long and is stored on seven computer diskettes.

This book is the product of five years of research, thought, and preparation by two academics, an expert on the Renaissance and a mathematician. In it we attempt to explain the notion of chance in simple language, intended for the average reader. The idea of chance is complex and elusive, but through essays that approach the idea from a wide variety of perspectives (see table of contents), we attempt to reveal its ultimate simplicity and unity.

Anecdotes from daily life, stories from newspapers, problems with grief and romance . . . these and other vignettes from daily life keep this book from being a scholarly study and should make it interesting for the man on the street who is curious and anxious about dealing with the age of uncertainty we are living in. It goes beyond the current best-seller *Megatrends* in that, instead of just describing a future full of uncertainty and flux, we recommend a point of view, a philosophy, which can help people live fuller and happier lives.

Our book is interdisciplinary in nature. It incorporates ideas from psychology, history, literature, economics, and politics, as well as the hard sciences, mathematics and physics. Conversations with people from all walks of life have convinced us that there is a vast potential readership for this book. Because of the pervasive nature of chance and uncertainty in today's world and the general level of ignorance of how to find happiness and deal with opportunities today, we believe that this book can become a guidebook for perplexed Americans in the 1980s. In this sense, it is a "self-help" book, well suited to the needs of today's readers.

The organization of the book is not completely revealed through its table of contents. It incorporates a very original randomizing device so that each reader will read the chapters of the book in a different order. This is something like a "choose your own plot" book, but entirely new and closely related to the theme of this book, chance.

We are interested in finding the best possible agent for this project, one who has contacts with some of the larger publishers, has been successful in getting books published, and believes that he or she can get *this book* published.

If you think you might be interested in pursuing this further, please write or call us. We would be happy to send you selected chapters, or the full book, or to come to talk to you in your offices.

Sincerely yours,

Catherine Lilly   Daniel Martin

ABOUT THE AUTHORS

Catherine Lilly, Ph.D. in mathematics, University of Michigan, 1971. Area of specialization: number theory. Currently Chairperson of Department of Mathematics at Westfield State College.

Daniel Martin, Ph.D. in Romance Languages and Literatures, Yale University, 1973. Author of a book on the notion of chance in French: *Montaigne et la Fortune: essai sur le hasard et le langage.* Paris: Honore Champion, 1977. At present, Associate Professor of French at the University of Massachusetts, Amherst.

TABLE OF CONTENTS
Unlocking Opportunity

1. The Return of Fortuna
2. Chance is Not Fate
3. Planning Versus Preparation
4. Mistakes
5. Opportunity
6. Coincidence
7. Time
8. Fortuna the Woman
9. Contingency Planning
10. Luck
11. The Wheel of Fortuna
12. The Mystery of Life
13. Randomness and Social Machines
14. Romantic Fortuna
15. Probability
16. Accident
17. The Politics of Fortuna
18. The Good Life
19. The Fortunate Individual
20. Let Us Know

ILLUSTRATION 11-2: William Hoffman

Mr. Geoff Miller
Editor
Los Angeles Magazine
1888 Century Park East
Los Angeles, CA 90067

Dear Mr. Miller:

I wonder if your magazine would like a story about John Soares, a resident of Orange County. For 10 years the colorful Soares was history's most successful crossroader (a crossroader is a person who cheats casinos), winning millions of dollars at craps, blackjack, and slot machines in gambling houses in Nevada and all over the world.

In the middle 1960s into the early 1970s, Soares and a Runyonesque crew of rogues (one was a beautiful woman, an icy calm ex-prostitute who alone collected more than 10,000 slot jackpots) were absolutely unstoppable. This article will reveal how they switched loaded dice into crap games right under the noses of big-time casino bosses, how they stacked entire shoes of cards without the blackjack dealer knowing, and how there wasn't a slot machine ever manufactured that they couldn't rig.

Eagle-eyed Mafia men ran many of the casinos when Soares operated, but they never caught him or his crew, nor did the local police or FBI. Soares, a sort of Robin Hood, is now a well-to-do California businessman. Never once, it should be repeated, was he caught, yet his pillage boggles the mind. The article, be assured, will be packed with adventure.

Although Soares was a crook, don't be surprised if many of your readers find themselves rooting for him.

I've written feature articles for numerous newspapers, including the *Baltimore News American*, the *St. Louis Globe Democrat*, the *Dallas Morning News*, and the *Washington Star*. I've also been published in such magazines as *Omni*, *True Detective*, and *Self*.

Sincerely yours,

William Hoffman

ILLUSTRATION 11-3: Elizabeth Tener

Ms. ————
Articles Editor
Major Woman's Magazine
Street Address
New York, NY 10022

Dear Ms. ————.

The last time I wrote for your magazine was in May 1985, when I worked with [another editor] on a story titled "———— ————
————." The other day I thought of your magazine again, while interviewing some "ex-druggie" teenagers for *Young Miss*. Would you be interested in a true-life story on parents who decided to put their teenage child in a treatment center for drug abusers?

The treatment center to which I refer—KIDS of Bergen County—is run by Dr. Miller Newton, a pioneer in teenage drug therapy and author of *Not My Kid: A Parent's Guide to Kids and Drugs*. It uses adolescent peer pressure and intensive family involvement to move druggie kids through a grueling four-step treatment and rehabilitation program. Along the way, the kids regain self-esteem and learn to substitute accomplishment and honest relationships for the instant "feel-good" sensations of the drug high. Recently I attended an open meeting at KIDS, where parents and kids confronted each other. I was very moved by the courage and honesty of those families who were trying valiantly to support the healing of their druggie kid and restore the family balance upset by the nightmare of drug use.

Besides being a powerful story in itself, such a family profile could be of value to your readers in many ways. They would learn to recognize a growing drug problem within their family; to realize that they are not to blame for their child's compulsion; to evaluate and choose professional help that delivers its money's worth; and to strengthen parenting skills—important even in families not touched by the drug problem. Dr. Newton has agreed to work closely with me on this piece. He knows of a number of families who would be delighted to tell their stories, and he can also supply referral information for the 25 or 30 best adolescent rehab facilities in the country.

As you know, adolescent drug abuse, already one of the most insidious, tragic, and widespread problems in the country, is worsening because of the

This query was written before *Young Miss* changed its name to *YM*.

falling prices of cocaine and the introduction of a smokeable form of it called "crack," which is almost instantly addictive. The "inside story" of a family's disrupted life might be a most effective way of wising up parents to the hidden danger and helping them to cope effectively.

[The author's bio has been omitted as she has previously sold to this publication; it appears in Chapter 5 as an illustration.] I'm enclosing a couple of stories I've already done on drugs. Let me know what you think. I hope to hear from you soon.

Sincerely yours,

Elizabeth Tener

ILLUSTRATION 11-4: Maxine Abrams

Medicine of the Future

New hope and help for the 10 (or 20) most common medical disorders—everything from heart disease and cancer to arthritis, diabetes, chronic depression, pulmonary disorders, kidney and stomach problems, visual and hearing disorders, infertility, and so on.

Top subspecialists in the fields of internal medicine, surgery, and psychiatry will be interviewed on imminent advances, plus the most promising *experimental* techniques and technologies already being offered patients today.

The medical and behavior sciences are expanding so rapidly that this article would require extensive research and would easily be long enough for a Good Housekeeping "book."

[The bio was omitted as Maxine Abrams has written for the magazine before. If she were submitting to a new magazine, her usual bio reads:

Maxine Abrams has specialized in medical writing and editing for the past 17 years. She has been a frequent contributor to *Good Housekeeping, Ladies' Home Journal, Harper's Bazaar,* and *Cosmopolitan.* Her work has also appeared in *New York Magazine, Parents' Magazine,* and the Sunday magazine of the *Philadelphia Inquirer.*

With Charles E. Flowers, Jr., M.D., she coauthored *A Woman Talks With Her Doctor,* published in hardcover by William Morrow and in paperback by Berkley Books. Excerpts appeared in *Cosmopolitan.* The book was also published abroad.

She lives in a suburb of Philadelphia and serves as editor and director of publications at The Medical College of Pennsylvania.]

ILLUSTRATION 11-5: Lisa Collier Cool

Mr. Peter Bloch
Managing Editor
Penthouse
1965 Broadway
New York, NY 10019

Dear Peter:

I thought your suggestion for a piece on Eurocurrency traders was an excellent idea, and now that I've looked into it, I'm even more convinced of the merit of the subject. The whole brokerage scene seems to be heating up quite a bit with all those revelations about check kiting and insider trading that keep coming out, creating considerable public interest in this subject.

Currency trading is where a lot of the financial action is right now. The volume of trading has almost doubled in the past six years—$50 billion a *day* in 1986 as compared to $5 billion in 1976. Currency traders are colorful characters—mostly young guys (under 35) who earn as much as $1 million a year and have the kind of upscale lifestyle that most of your readers only fantasize about. One broker told me that a trader who earned a mere $200,000 in commissions would be considered a failure and transferred into some other division of the brokerage house or bank.

I was thinking of titling the piece "The Fastest Game in Town" and focusing on such points as how traders get into the field, how currency trading works, what the scene and lifestyle are like (my sources tell me these guys wake up at 4 A.M. to call in for quotes on yen and marks), the training and pressure of the jobs, and exactly what this subculture is really like, with plenty of quotes and anecdotes from people in the field.

I've long wanted to write for *Penthouse,* as I've always enjoyed the lively articles you run, and will hope for a go-ahead from you.

Sincerely yours,

Lisa Collier Cool

ILLUSTRATION 11-6: Robert Elgin

Dear _____:

Perhaps an illustration or two might best describe the plight of thousands of exotic animals that are declared surplus by zoos or independent animal breeders each year.

In September 1982, one lion, two jaguars, one leopard, two wolves, and five Dall sheep were given to an animal dealer by the Des Moines zoo coordinator. Despite the fact that all the cats were highly trained, they were all, excepting one, shot at close range with a heavy tranquilizer rifle (with barbed darts) and loaded into spaces in the dealer's converted camper truck that would not permit them to turn around. One wolf was so mistreated when the tranquilizer failed to put her under that the zoo curator intervened. The veterinarian, who was present to sign the necessary health certificate, was later questioned by U.S. Department of Agriculture officers and confirmed that none of the compartments the animals were placed in would begin to meet USDA minimum standards.

When one zookeeper later asked the zoo coordinator where the animals had gone and whether they'd arrived safely, she was told that any animals that had left the zoo were no longer any concern of hers and that she should examine her emotional attitude and determine whether she was suited for zoo work.

The USDA, in its subsequent investigation, found some of the animals in a small exhibit in Arkansas. The zoo staff (the keepers) feel, however, that the lion was probably sold to a shooting preserve and killed by a "big game hunter" for a trophy. This is the fate of many surplus exotics.

Some years ago we gave five young wolves to an animal dealer we trusted. He promised that the wolves would be given to responsible friends of his who had large private zoos. I was later informed by a friend (a field agent for the U.S. Department of the Interior) that the wolves had been sold at the infamous Cape Girardeau auction. They further traced the wolves to North Carolina, where they had been sold as pets. Perhaps this is a better fate than four other wolves met in Iowa just two years ago. They were killed and skinned, and their pelts were sold in Chicago.

Literally thousands of animals are auctioned at Cape Girardeau, Missouri, each year, with millions of dollars changing hands. Some, undoubtedly, are purchased by ranchers who use the hooved animals to improve their herds; others, such as the predator cats, are purchased by the very, very few people who are capable of handling them and who can provide proper facilities. The rest, the vast majority, are sold to be shot for trophies or end up as pets for individuals who have no idea how to care for them.

One of our local USDA agents informed me yesterday that three exotic animal auctions are to be held in Iowa next month. Last week I received a call from a veterinarian requesting advice on the care and training of a young lioness who'd been brought to his clinic. This morning another man called me to inquire what he should do with a six-month-old cougar he bought two days ago from an animal dealer in Iowa. The cougar appeared to have feline distemper and will probably die.

The situation is so appalling, so widespread, and so little known to most animal lovers that I feel something must be done. The American Association of Zoological Parks and Aquariums frowns on the practice, as do most individual zoo directors. In reality, however, many turn their heads and simply give the animals away to unscrupulous dealers knowing full well what their fate will be. After all, few zoo directors wish to face the outcry and horror the Detroit Zoo went through when they put some surplus tigers to death last year.

Apparently most of the humane societies prefer to avoid the problem. It will, however, be a big item on the agenda of the national meeting next September of the American Association of Zoological Parks and Aquariums. Whatever action that group may take, however, will do nothing to interfere with the conduct of the many independent dealers who will continue to obtain animals for killing or sale to persons who lack the ability to care for them.

My daughter, Becky, is considered an authority on the care and handling of captive wolves. She presented a paper at the first International Symposium on Captive Wolves, in Flint, Michigan, in October 1981. Just two days before the symposium convened, a youngster was killed by a captive wolf in Detroit. Three years ago a pet wolf slashed his owner's face to ribbons at a vet clinic here. This next week two beautiful lions and two tigers will depart from the Des Moines Zoo—destination a secret. Probably they will be shot.

Friends of mine in the USDA and the USDI have attempted to control this situation for years—with only limited success. Last fall, a U.S. senator attempted to prevent USDA agents from inspecting animals and cages at Cape Girardeau. The USDA is sending me a complete list of all transactions there. I also plan to work with USDI agents in Nebraska, Missouri, and Iowa. Several zoo directors will be involved.

From 1967 to 1982, I was director of the Des Moines Zoo, where I originated a system of training wild animals to adapt effectively to captivity. I describe this approach and other aspects of zoo management in my two published books, *Man in a Cage* (Iowa State University Press, 1972) and *The Tiger is My Brother* (William Morrow and Company, under movie option).

Yours truly,

Bob Elgin

ILLUSTRATION 11-7: Susan Lapinski

Idea for *Parade*

Five years ago, a multimillionaire industrialist named Eugene Lang was about to give the commencement address to a bunch of sixth graders at his alma mater, P.S. 121 in East Harlem. He was going to tell them that hard work pays off and that if they followed his lead, they could be millionaires, too.

But at the last minute, the wealthy businessman scrapped that hackneyed sort of Horatio Alger speech. Instead, he decided to give his audience of black and Hispanic students and their impoverished families something tangible to hope for and hold on to. He told them that if the students stayed in school, he would pay the college tuitions for each of them. The audience gasped, then mobbed Lang, cheering him and kissing him.

Now, 5 years later, 50 of the 62 graduates of P.S. 121 are still in the New York area, and 47 of them are still in school. At least half the kids have grades good enough to take advantage of the industrialist's generous offer. They've been studying hard and benefiting from the coaching of an educational consultant, hired by the industrialist to guide his protégés.

The bare bones of this story were recently reported in *The New York Times.* For *Parade,* I'd do a warm, personal interest kind of story, focusing on the industrialist and some of the students who are benefiting from his philanthropy.

What made Eugene Lang reach deep into his own pocket to help some kids he didn't know? How has the promise of a free college education and the support of somebody like Lang affected a young man like David Nieves?

"My parents are dropouts," David says. "They want me to go all the way now."

This story has the potential to warm hearts and maybe move some minds, too. I'd love to write it for *Parade*.

(30)

Chapter 12

Power Querying

Five hundred dollars, $1,000, $2,500, $3,000, $4,000! Did these article prices mentioned in the previous chapter surprise you? Were you thinking as you looked over the queries, "I could have written this one—and maybe that one"? Perhaps you're now wondering whether there's some secret I failed to tell you that explains why these fairly ordinary-sounding queries sold for such high sums. Or maybe you're saying, "Well, if I had as many credits as those authors do, editors would be beating down the door to buy my work, too. But how do you get to there from here?"

Here's how:

Think Big From the Start.   The best query topics are those that would appeal to a large audience, say one million or more readers. While both "How to Crochet a Baby Layette" and "How to Raise Your Baby's IQ" are potentially saleable topics, the second idea would be likely to sell for about ten times the price of the first, because just about any new parent would be interested in this subject.

Thinking big also entails familiarizing yourself with the best-paying publications that are likely to run the kind of articles you'd like to write. Although I've previously suggested that you read at least one issue of any publication you are aiming for, an even better strategy is to *subscribe* to five or six of the most promising magazines and study them in depth each month—even after you've sold a piece or two to one of them.

Make Work Your Hobby. What I mean by this is that you should be building your freelance career twenty-four hours a day. A dream could trigger an idea; casual contacts you make at cocktail parties could be turned into potential profile subjects or interview sources; skimming the morning paper could become research as you start clipping all items of even marginal interest; and time spent in lines or commuting could be used to record ideas, jot down interesting phrases, or even compose leads for new queries. A total immersion in their work is typical of most highly successful authors I know.

Set Goals and Exceed Them. When I was a full-time agent, I set the goal of selling three books every month. If I sold six books one month, the following month's goal would still be three; extras are just a bonus. Now that I spend most of my time writing, my goal is to sell one of my own books each year and one of my articles each month. I am firmly convinced that having a specific (and reasonably attainable) goal psychologically pushes you to greater heights.

Naturally, if you find that you are consistently exceeding my recommended goal of one new query a week, one new sale a month, raise the goals until they are slightly above your current level of performance.

Be Your Own Cheerleader. Writing is a lonely business, and it's natural to turn to your friends or spouse for support. However, I find that this is a poor idea. First of all, those in your social circle are unlikely to be knowledgeable about today's publishing scene and therefore can't offer constructive advice. Furthermore, they may sabotage your efforts by reacting less enthusiastically than you'd hoped, either out of misconceptions about the market or unconscious envy of your new career.

My philosophy is that my opinion is the only one that counts. If I think I've got a good idea, rather than confide in friends, I ask an authority—an editor at a magazine—via a query letter. I ignore rejections, too; I've developed a thick skin from years of starting my day as an agent with a stack of rejections. I keep trying to sell my ideas until I either get a contract or lose interest in the project.

Make Submissions a Priority. Getting an idea is a little like starting a love affair: the excitement is highest when you first meet.

When you get an idea, get to work immediately gathering any necessary research. As soon as you've typed it up, mail it off right away. Otherwise, the passion may fade and the query will have a less-than-ardent tone that may undermine your sales efforts.

I don't think it's worth slaving over a query too long. I don't mean you should do a sloppy job—accuracy and a smooth style are very important—but that you should stop before you edit out all your enthusiasm. Once your query seems reasonably good, send it out. Most top writers write their queries in a casual, almost offhand style that seems to suggest that the idea is going directly from their brain to that of the editor.

If You Can Sell One, You Can Sell More. One of the keys to a steady income is to find steady customers who will buy your articles frequently. When you are first starting, you'll want to cast as wide a net as possible, by submitting a variety of ideas to many different publications. Once you find three or four receptive publications, your objective should be to exploit these markets as efficiently as possible, first by offering new ideas that are somewhat similar to those they've bought before to maximize the prospects of a second sale, and then by branching out into different kinds of writing that will encourage your editor to think of you for his or her own ideas

Keep Alert for Opportunities to Upgrade. My grandfather used to say, "Don't let the nickel in front of your eyes blind you to the half dollar in the distance." Once you get in with a magazine, it's easy to fall into the trap of not looking beyond the next raise. But if you're now making five hundred dollars an article, it might be possible to jump to one thousand dollars by selling to a slightly better publication—then to turn around and get twelve hundred dollars from the magazine you currently write for.

Another good way to upgrade is to consider whether any of the articles you sell has any potential to be expanded into a book. This book, for example, started out as a *Writer's Digest* magazine piece on queries. With your published article as a sample, all you'd have to do is develop a chapter outline (and your article could be one of the chapters, if you've retained book rights) and a query or proposal.

Develop a Winning Image. There are lots of subtle ways you can make editors think of you as a professional right from the start

Attractive letterhead stationery is a good investment. (But don't describe yourself as a writer on the letterhead; editors consider this a sure sign of an amateur at work.) Next, sign and return article contracts promptly, deliver your pieces one week ahead of the deadline to demonstrate your reliability, and make sure your research is first-rate.

Whenever you write or call your editor, try to work in a reference or two to something that appeared in a recent issue to subtly highlight your great familiarity with the magazine. Drop occasional references to your other sales to signal how much demand there is for your work. From time to time, send a published piece along with your new queries to regular customers—this will make the point even more effectively.

Use Networking.   Once you've begun to establish yourself, it's useful to get to know other professional writers through a writer's organization. The American Society of Journalists and Authors is open to writers who've published two books or eight articles in the past two years; various combinations of credits are also acceptable. The group puts out a newsletter and offers a variety of services. Call or write the society at 1501 Broadway, Suite 1907, New York, NY 10036, (212) 997-0947, for detailed information.

Local writers' groups are fun, but not necessarily productive sources of insider information. The best groups are composed only of working journalists or successful magazine freelancers, who are in a position to trade tips with you on good editors and publications for different projects.

Try to Sell a Column.   If you are writing three or more articles a year for one magazine, suggest periodically that they give you a regular column. Study the magazine closely to detect any chinks in its coverage of topics likely to interest their group of readers, then propose that you write a monthly column on the topic. Being a columnist not only provides steady income but will impress other editors you query.

Another suggestion to make from time to time with your regular customers is that they name you a contributing editor. While there's no cash advantage to this at most magazines, it solidifies your relationship, gets your name before the public (on the masthead), and sounds good when you contact other publications.

Write Longer Articles. Many magazines run both features (short articles, generally less than two thousand five hundred words) and articles (longer pieces, usually four thousand words and up). Since magazines pay more for their articles than for their features and attach more importance to the major pieces, it makes sense to establish yourself as a writer of articles, rather than of features, at magazines that make this distinction. You'll get more respect—and more cash.

It's easier to write one long article of four thousand words than two features of two thousand words apiece. Why? Very little additional research is required for a longer piece than for a shorter one: since all your research will be on the same topic, you won't be wandering all over the library looking for unrelated topics. The writing is easier, too: you only need one lead (which I find to be the most time-consuming paragraph of the piece) and you have the room to develop your ideas in greater depth. And, best of all, you have half the marketing work, and a more impressive clip to show for your efforts.

Pick Up Your Writing Pace. Write twice as fast and you'll make twice as much money. When I first started writing, I used to labor over each sentence before I went on to the next, which resulted in a very low hourly pay rate. Now I quickly zip out a rough draft, *then* polish later. Working directly at the typewriter, instead of doing the first draft in longhand, will also accelerate your writing speed, since your first draft may be good enough to submit.

A word processor will speed your writing even more, since you never have to retype. You just insert new text in the proper place, delete material you don't like, and let the computer rearrange the pages for a perfect manuscript. Word processors can also check your spelling, do word counts, and even suggest words to use.

You'll also write faster if you develop a rigid writing schedule; three hours a day is enough to turn out writing in volume. Train yourself to work on cue, without lengthy warm-up routines. Inspiration can be trained to arrive on command if you follow your routine religiously.

Get More Mileage Out of Each Idea. Why stop with one sale when the same idea could be sold several times to noncompeting markets? If your idea is currently slanted to women's magazines, consider whether a slight change in emphasis might make it right for the men's magazine marketplace, too. Or your idea could work for both adults and teens with minor changes. Use your imagination to develop more markets for each idea.

After you've turned a query into a sale, consider also marketing second serial rights to your published piece if you haven't assigned them to the first magazine. Consult *Writer's Market* for a list of likely magazines, newspaper syndicates, or Sunday supplements, and invest a few bucks in stamps. The result could be hundreds or even thousands in additional income for work you've already been paid for once.

Believe That the Best Is Yet to Come. Although the right attitude is important in most professions, in writing it's doubly vital because each word you write reflects your inner feelings about yourself. Once you truly believe in your ultimate success, your work will echo this positive perception and project the confident air that attracts editors.

THE ULTIMATE GOAL—NO MORE QUERIES

The more successful a freelancer becomes, the fewer queries he or she writes. Once you've entered the inner circle of big-money magazine writers, you'll find that the editors start querying *you* with their ideas. The reputation you've established by following the steps recommended in this book will land you those two-thousand-dollar, four-thousand-dollar, and even ten-thousand-dollar assignments.

Excelsior!

A Letter to the Reader

I am not currently looking for literary agency clients or able to offer editorial services of any kind. But I'd be interested in learning what sort of results you have with my method or hearing your comments on my book.

If you'd like to write me, use the address below. Include an SASE if you'd like a reply. Best of luck with your writing.

Best wishes,

Lisa Collier Cool
% Writer's Digest Books
1507 Dana Ave.
Cincinnati, OH 45207

Index

Abrams, Maxine, 112, 121
Agents
    contracts with, 108
    example of, 80-81
    queries to, 75-79
Anecdotes, 28-29, 38
Article fees, 107
"As told to" articles, 6
Author's bio, 46-53
    example of, 54

Background, 39
Book contracts, 107-108
Book queries, 75-79
    examples of, 80-87
    slants for, 16
    submissions of, 98-99

"Call of the wild" slants, 18
Career advice, 7-8
Case histories, see *anecdotes*
Closing paragraphs, 65-66
Comparisons, 30
Contracts, 102-103, 106-109
    book, 107-108
    magazine, 102-107
    sample, 104-105
    with agents, 108
Covering letters, 65-66, 68-69, 72, 76
Crime articles, 9

Delivery date, 77

Editors, 96-97
Editing, 63-67
    of author's bio, 53
    of leads, 32-33
    of summaries, 43
Elgin, Bob, 113, 123-125
Evergreens, 10
Exhibits, 78
Exposes, 8
Extras, 42-43

Facts, 30, 37, 55-62, 91

Five Ws, 26-27
Foreword, 77
Format for books, 77-78
Formats for queries, 67-68, 72-74, 88-89
Foster, Rory C., 80-81
Future, 39-40

"Gee whiz" slants, 21-22
Geography, as slant, 20

Hoffman, William, 111, 119
How-to articles, 7
Humor, 21

Ideas, 4-12
Illustrations, 41, 77
Inspirational articles, 10
Interviews, 6, 57-59
Inverted pyramid, 27-28

Lapinski, Susan, 114, 126-127
Lead paragraphs, 25-33
    examples of, 28-31
    mistakes to avoid in, 31-32
Length of query, 63-64, 75
Library research, 56-57, 59-61
Lifestyle articles, 9-10
Lilly, Catherine, 110, 115-117
Literary Marketplace, 98

Magazine queries, see *queries*
Mailing of queries, 100
Markets, 92-93, 94-96
Martin, Daniel, 110, 115-117
Medical articles, 9
Money slants, 17-18
Multiple idea queries, 68
Multiple submissions, 99-100

Negative phrasing, 89-90
"New and improved" slants, 16-17
News pegs, 41
Numbers (in slanting), 20
"Nuts and bolts," 39, 76-78

Opening paragraphs, see *lead paragraphs*
Outline, 36-37

Personal experience articles, 4-6
Personal finance, 8
Positioning, 22
Profile articles, 6
Proofreading, 66-67, 91
Promises, 19
Publishers Weekly, 79

Queries
  common mistakes, 88-93
  samples, 13, 23, 34-35, 44-45, 70-71, 72-74, 80-87, 110-133
  when not to use, 2
Questions, 29-30
Quotes, 30-31, 38

Reader, 40
  visualizing readers, 95-96
Rejections, 97-98
Relationship articles, 8
Research, 55-57, 59-62, 78-79, 91
Reversal, in slanting, 19, 23

SASE, 92
Scare tactics, 19
Science articles, 9
Seasonal topics, 7
Secrets, 19

Self-help articles, 7
Sex articles, 8
Sexy slants, 17
Slants, 14-22, 24
  definition of, 14
  examples of, 16-22
Sources, 37-38
Statement of purpose, 36
Submissions, 94-103, 129-130
  finding markets, 94-96
  multiple, 99-100
Summaries, 36-43
  example of, 44-45
Sunshine-Genova, Amy, 29-30, 34-35

Tener, Elizabeth, 54, 111, 119-120
Themes, 39
Timing, 40-41
Titles, 22, 24
Travel, 10, 20-21
A Treasury of Tips for the Writer, 25-26

Volunteer Lawyers for the Arts, 108

Writer, The, 95
Writer's Digest, 95
Writer's Handbook, 95, 98
Writer's Market, 92, 95, 98, 101, 108
Writing credits, 50-52
Word count, 76-77

About the Author

Lisa Collier Cool was a literary agent for fifteen years. Now a full-time freelancer, she is presently a contributing editor to *Cosmopolitan* and the author of more than 100 articles to newspapers and such magazines as *Harper's, Glamour, Family Circle, Modern Bride, Playgirl,* and *Publishers Weekly.* She has taught writing at Parsons School of Design in New York City and is a member of the American Society of Journalists and Authors.

More Great Books
For Writers!

1996 Writer's Market—Celebrating 75 years of helping writers realize their dreams, this newest edition contains information on 4,000 writing opportunities. You'll find all the facts vital to the success of your writing career, including an up-to-date listing of buyers of books, articles and stories, listings of contests and awards, plus articles and interviews with top professionals. *#10432/$27.99/1008 pages*

Writer's Encyclopedia, Third Edition—Rediscover this popular writer's reference—now with information about electronic resources, plus more than 100 new entries. You'll find facts, figures, definitions and examples designed to answer questions about every discipline connected with writing and help you convey a professional image. *#10464/$22.99/560 pages/62 b&w illus.*

Discovering the Writer Within: 40 Days to More Imaginative Writing—Uncover the creative individual inside who will, with encouragement, turn secret thoughts and special moments into enduring words. You'll learn how to find something exciting in unremarkable places, write punchy first sentences for imaginary stories, give a voice to inanimate objects and much more! *#10472/$14.99/192 pages/paperback*

How to Write Attention-Grabbing Query & Cover Letters—Use the secrets Wood reveals to write queries perfectly tailored, too good to turn down! In this guidebook, you will discover why boldness beats blandness in queries every time, ten basics you *must* have in your article queries, ten query blunders that can destroy publication chances and much more. *#10462/$17.99/208 pages*

The Writer's Legal Guide, Revised Edition—Now the answer to all your legal questions is right at your fingertips! The updated version of this treasured desktop companion contains essential information on business issues, copyright protection and registration, contract negotiation, income taxation, electronic rights and much, much more. *#10478/$19.95/256 pages/paperback*

Writing to Sell—You'll discover high-quality writing and marketing counsel in this classic writing guide from well-known agent Scott Meredith. His timeless advice will guide you along the professional writing path as you get help with creating characters, plotting a novel, placing your work, formatting a manuscript, deciphering a publishing contract—even combating a slump! *#10476/$17.99/240 pages*

Writing for Money—Discover where to look for writing opportunities—and how to make them pay off. You'll learn how to write for magazines, newspapers, radio and TV, newsletters, greeting cards and a dozen other hungry markets! *#10425/$17.99/256 pages*